The Politics and Science of COVID-19

Other Books in the Current Controversies Series

Attacks on Science
Big Tech and Democracy
The Capitol Riot: Fragile Democracy
Cyberterrorism
Domestic Extremism
Domestic vs. Offshore Manufacturing
Fossil Fuel Industries and the Green Economy
Hate Groups
The Internet of Things
Libertarians, Socialists, and Other Third Parties
Reparations for Black Americans
Sustainable Consumption

Current **CONTROVERSIES**

The Politics and Science of COVID-19

Lisa Idzikowski, Book Editor

GREENHAVEN
PUBLISHING

Published in 2022 by Greenhaven Publishing, LLC
353 3rd Avenue, Suite 255, New York, NY 10010

Copyright © 2022 by Greenhaven Publishing, LLC

First Edition

Articles in Greenhaven Publishing anthologies are often edited for length to meet page
requirements. In addition, original titles of these works are changed to clearly present
the main thesis and to explicitly indicate the author's opinion. Every effort is made to
ensure that Greenhaven Publishing accurately reflects the original intent of the authors.
Every effort has been made to trace the owners of the copyrighted material.

Cover image: Matt Gush/Shutterstock.com

Library of Congress Cataloging-in-Publication Data

Names: Idzikowski, Lisa, editor.
Title: The politics and science of COVID-19 / Lisa Idzikowski, book editor.
Description: First edition. | New York : Greenhaven Publishing,
2022. | Series: Current controversies | Includes index.
Identifiers: ISBN 9781534508620 (library binding) | ISBN
9781534508613 (paperback) | ISBN 9781534508637 (ebook)
Subjects: LCSH: COVID-19 (Disease). | COVID-19 (Disease)--
Political aspects. | COVID-19 (Disease)--Social aspects.
Classification: LCC RA644.C67 P655 2022 | DDC 614.5'92414--dc23

Manufactured in the United States of America

Website: http://greenhavenpublishing.com

Contents

Foreword   **11**

Introduction   **14**

Chapter 1: Was the United States Prepared for a Pandemic?

Overview: Could the US Have Been Better Prepared for the COVID-19 Pandemic?   **19**

Wayne Lewis

The author examines why it appears that the United States was caught off guard. It is difficult at best to prepare for a disease outbreak when a virus is completely new. On the other hand, many protocols are universal.

Yes: The United States Was Prepared for a Pandemic

A "Pandemic Playbook" Prepared by the Previous Administration Was Available to Consult   **23**

Victoria Knight

Contrary to some reports, Obama administration staffers prepared a detailed report on how to respond to a possible threat to the US. The report provided plans on how to act against a variety of threats, including pandemics. The availability of this plan was denied by Republicans supporting President Trump.

US Schools Quickly Pivoted to Online Learning During Lockdown   **26**

Anya Kamenetz

The COVID pandemic made online learning a must for most students in the US. Schools, students, teachers, and parents were caught up in a storm of change at the drop of a hat. Some families made the transition easily, others not so well.

Medical Professionals Shattered the Illusion That the US Was Ready for an Outbreak   **33**

Nikhila Natarajan

The public heard from many during the COVID-19 pandemic. Doctors, politicians, nurses, respiratory specialists, teachers, grocery store workers, and so many others. Some of these people became the storytellers of the pandemic. Through their stories, they helped others during the historic pandemic.

No: The United States Was Not Well Prepared for the COVID-19 Pandemic

Government Failed to Keep the US Prepared for COVID   37

Daniel M. Gerstein

For many years, presidential administrations have made preparations for health emergencies. The Trump administration ignored previous preparedness protocols and suggested it was not the responsibility of the federal government to be in charge during COVID-19.

PPE Shortages Revealed the
US Government's Lack of Preparedness   43

Tucker Doherty and Brianna Ehley

It is shameful that during the height of the pandemic President Trump repeatedly claimed that the shortage of PPE across the US was "fake news." Why would hospital staff intentionally lie about the tools and medical equipment they needed to combat the virus?

The White House Disregarded Its Own Pandemic Experts   47

Ana Maria Lankford, Derrick Storzieri, and Joseph Fitsanakis

The intelligence components of the federal government's Biological Defense Program offered actionable forewarning about an impending pandemic, yet senior US government officials repeatedly claimed that the virus "came out of nowhere."

Chapter 2: Are Science and Politics at Odds with One Another?

Overview: Politicians Should Not Dismiss Science   71

Mauktik Kulkarni

Science seeks to uncover truths and facts. Politics does not. The US was not the only country in the world where politicians acted against the advice of scientists during the COVID-19 pandemic.

Yes: Science and Politics Are at Odds with One Another

Deadly Lies Were the Norm in the 2020 Pandemic   74

Daniel Funke and Katie Sanders

Science and medical experts are summarily dismissed in favor of misinformation and outright lies promulgated by online hucksters,

TV personalities, QAnon fraudsters, radio opinionators, medical posers, and even government personnel and politicians.

What Happens When We Prioritize Politics and Economics Over Science   **84**

Meridith McGraw and Nancy Cook

What was happening at the White House as the COVID-19 pandemic began to take shape in the US? President Trump appeared more interested in the stock market and other economic indicators instead of the warnings from medical experts and advisers.

QAnon Conspiracy Theories Fight Against Science   **89**

Marc-André Argentino

The QAnon phenomenon began in 2017 and continues to push wild conspiracy theories. This group is a threat to public health because it has caused individuals to cling to lies and misinformation instead of looking to advice of health experts and scientists.

No: At Times Science Works with or Around Politics

The Science-Policy Interface Can Be Improved by Integrating Scientific Investigation with Political Debate   **93**

Peter Horton and Garrett W. Brown

There is currently intense debate over expertise, evidence, and "post-truth" politics. The authors put forward a methodology for evidence-based policy making intended as a way of helping navigate this web of complexity.

Waiving Intellectual Property Protections Is Key to Fighting the Pandemic Around the World   **104**

Daniel Takash

Biden's plans to ship 60 million doses of the vaccine and required materials to India as that country faced one of the deadliest outbreaks of the pandemic will supercharge the fight across the world.

Science Diplomats Can Facilitate Multilateral Responses to Global Challenges   **107**

Lorenzo Melchor

The COVID-19 crisis has shown how countries initially responded to a global challenge on their own, instead of relying on a multilateral, science diplomacy–based response. Science diplomacy sits across national borders, policy frameworks, and stakeholders of all natures and professional backgrounds.

Chapter 3: Does Politics Influence Medical Treatment During a Pandemic?

Overview: The COVID-19 Pandemic Underscored the Inequities in Healthcare **114**

N. Jensen, A. H. Kelly, and M. Avendano

In this excerpted viewpoint, the authors argue that the COVID-19 pandemic exposed and exacerbated health disparities and their underlying social determinants in the US and globally. Scrutiny of the pandemic could help address structural conditions at their root.

Yes: Politics Does Influence Medical Treatments During a Pandemic

Despite Warnings from Medical Experts, the President Touted Ineffective Treatments **119**

The Hindu

Despite warnings from medical experts, President Trump endorsed treatments for COVID-19 infections that proved ineffective and even dangerous. Again and again, Trump proved his unwillingness to let scientific and medical experts take the lead.

Science Denial Hampered the Pandemic Response **121**

Adam Wernick

Former president Donald Trump and many conservatives deny climate change and the science surrounding the complicated issue. Is it any surprise then that these same people denied the severity of the coronavirus?

No: Factors Besides Politics Influence Medical Treatments During a Pandemic

Scientists in the US and China Collaborated to Fight COVID **126**

Jenny J. Lee and John P. Haupt

Politics played an outsize role in the coronavirus pandemic. Former president Donald Trump went so far as to refer to the virus as the "China virus" on numerous occasions. Yet scientists across the world have continued or in some cases increased their level of collaboration. Significantly, statistics show this happened between scientists and researchers in the US and China.

Foundations Must Help Native American Communities
During COVID   **129**

Heidi A. Schultz

Even in the best of times, Native Americans living on government
land face challenging everyday living situations. The COVID-19
pandemic highlighted the stress and strains that Native American
communities face directly. The author points out how foundations
should be helping these vulnerable communities.

Chapter 4: Can the Impact of Pandemics Be Changed for the Future?

Overview: How to Prevent Future Pandemics   **134**

Marisa Peyre, Flavie Luce Goutard, and François Roger

Can pandemics be prevented in the future? Some organizations
are working to do just that. Researchers know that the chance of
more pandemics occurring in the future is almost assured, and they
understand outbreaks are likely to start with animals. Consequently,
these agencies have outlined steps that suggest quick, global
cooperation and action when the next pandemic looms.

Yes: The Impact of Pandemics Can Be Changed for the Future

Rapid Response Is Key When Battling Public Health
Issues   **140**

*Centers for Disease Control, Global Rapid
Response Team*

One of the keys to controlling public health issues is to act quickly.
The CDC's Rapid Response Team does just that. Many individuals in
the group are ready at a moment's notice to go anywhere in the world
to help when a disease outbreak occurs. They stopped Ebola from
becoming a pandemic, and this knowledge is ready to use against
future possible pandemics.

Researchers' Understanding of Viruses Allows for Vaccine
Development at Astonishing Speed   **143**

Anthony King

The author gives a balanced and technical look at the development
of potential vaccines making a path to fight against the coronavirus
pandemic, explaining the basics of virus types and how they are used
to procure vaccines.

Build on What's Been Learned from COVID-19 to Prepare
for the Next Pandemic   148

   Tiffany A. Radcliff and Angela Clendenin

   Disasters like the COVID-19 pandemic can provide important
   lessons for the next time around. Ongoing innovation that builds on
   rapid adoption of technologies around COVID-19 will help people
   adjust to sudden lifestyle changes when the next pandemic strikes.

No: Changing the Impact of Future Pandemics Is Very Challenging

Mistrust of Science Fuels Chaos During a Pandemic   153

   Martha Molfetas

   The US has a science denial problem that impinges on two important
   issues: emerging infectious diseases and climate change. Some see
   the two as inextricably intertwined. Countries that put their trust in
   science have done a better job in battling COVID-19 than countries
   ignoring science.

Vaccine Hesitancy Prevents Herd Immunity Against
Pandemics   156

   Kelly Elterman

   When people don't trust vaccines, it can take much longer to reach
   herd immunity, which is so important when a pandemic is raging
   through a population. Why do people fear vaccines, and what can be
   done to convince them that the vaccines made to fight COVID are
   safe and effective?

Partisan Politics Erodes Trust in the World Health
Organization   163

   J. J. Moncus and Aidan Connaughton

   During the global pandemic, WHO played its role as the global
   watchdog and adviser. Unfortunately, when President Trump
   criticized WHO early in the pandemic, his Republican base accepted
   his ideas. Consequently, a large percentage of them do not trust the
   actions of WHO.

Organizations to Contact   166
Bibliography   170
Index   173

Foreword

"Controversy" is a word that has an undeniably unpleasant connotation. It carries a definite negative charge. Controversy can spoil family gatherings, spread a chill around classroom and campus discussion, inflame public discourse, open raw civic wounds, and lead to the ouster of public officials. We often feel that controversy is almost akin to bad manners, a rude and shocking eruption of that which must not be spoken or thought of in polite, tightly guarded society. To avoid controversy, to quell controversy, is often seen as a public good, a victory for etiquette, perhaps even a moral or ethical imperative.

Yet the studious, deliberate avoidance of controversy is also a whitewashing, a denial, a death threat to democracy. It is a false sterilizing and sanitizing and superficial ordering of the messy, ragged, chaotic, at times ugly processes by which a healthy democracy identifies and confronts challenges, engages in passionate debate about appropriate approaches and solutions, and arrives at something like a consensus and a broadly accepted and supported way forward. Controversy is the megaphone, the speaker's corner, the public square through which the citizenry finds and uses its voice. Controversy is the life's blood of our democracy and absolutely essential to the vibrant health of our society.

Our present age is certainly no stranger to controversy. We are consumed by fierce debates about technology, privacy, political correctness, poverty, violence, crime and policing, guns, immigration, civil and human rights, terrorism, militarism, environmental protection, and gender and racial equality. Loudly competing voices are raised every day, shouting opposing opinions, putting forth competing agendas, and summoning starkly different visions of a utopian or dystopian future. Often these voices attempt to shout the others down; there is precious little listening and considering among the cacophonous din. Yet listening and considering, too, are essential to the health of a democracy. If controversy is democracy's lusty lifeblood, respectful listening and careful thought are its higher faculties, its brain, its conscience.

Current Controversies does not shy away from or attempt to hush the loudly competing voices. It seeks to provide readers with as wide and representative as possible a range of articulate voices on any given controversy of the day, separates each one out to allow it to be heard clearly and fairly, and encourages careful listening to each of these well-crafted, thoughtfully expressed opinions, supplied by some of today's leading academics, thinkers, analysts, politicians, policy makers, economists, activists, change agents, and advocates. Only after listening to a wide range of opinions on an issue, evaluating the strengths and weaknesses of each argument, assessing how well the facts and available evidence mesh with the stated opinions and conclusions, and thoughtfully and critically examining one's own beliefs and conscience can the reader begin to arrive at his or her own conclusions and articulate his or her own stance on the spotlighted controversy.

This process is facilitated and supported in each Current Controversies volume by an introduction and chapter overviews that provide readers with the essential context they need to begin engaging with the spotlighted controversies, with the debates surrounding them, and with their own perhaps shifting or nascent opinions on them. Chapters are organized around several key questions that are answered with diverse opinions representing all points on the political spectrum. In its content, organization, and methodology, readers are encouraged to determine the authors' point of view and purpose, interrogate and analyze the various arguments and their rhetoric and structure, evaluate the arguments' strengths and weaknesses, test their claims against available facts and evidence, judge the validity of the reasoning, and bring into clearer, sharper focus the reader's own beliefs and conclusions and how they may differ from or align with those in the collection or those of classmates.

Research has shown that reading comprehension skills improve dramatically when students are provided with compelling, intriguing, and relevant "discussable" texts. The subject matter of these collections could not be more compelling, intriguing, or urgently relevant to today's students and the world they are poised to inherit. The anthologized articles also provide the basis for stimulating, lively, and passionate classroom debates. Students who are compelled to anticipate objections to their own argument and identify the flaws in those of an opponent read more carefully, think more critically, and steep themselves in relevant context, facts, and information more thoroughly. In short, using discussable text of the kind provided by every single volume in the Current Controversies series encourages close reading, facilitates reading comprehension, fosters research, strengthens critical thinking, and greatly enlivens and energizes classroom discussion and participation. The entire learning process is deepened, extended, and strengthened.

If we are to foster a knowledgeable, responsible, active, and engaged citizenry, we must provide readers with the intellectual, interpretive, and critical-thinking tools and experience necessary to make sense of the world around them and of the all-important debates and arguments that inform it. We must encourage them not to run away from or attempt to quell controversy but to embrace it in a responsible, conscientious, and thoughtful way, to sharpen and strengthen their own informed opinions by listening to and critically analyzing those of others. This series encourages respectful engagement with and analysis of current controversies and competing opinions and fosters a resulting increase in the strength and rigor of one's own opinions and stances. As such, it helps readers assume their rightful place in the public square and provides them with the skills necessary to uphold their awesome responsibility—guaranteeing the continued and future health of a vital, vibrant, and free democracy.

Introduction

"The biggest takeaway about US public opinion in the first year of the coronavirus outbreak may be the extent to which the decidedly nonpartisan virus met with an increasingly partisan response. America's partisan divide stood out even by international standards: No country was as politically divided over its government's handling of the outbreak."

—Pew Research Center

On February 11, 2020, the World Health Organization (WHO) took steps and declared that the disease caused by the novel coronavirus SARS-CoV-2 be named COVID-19. An important distinction of this novel virus is that it is a new disease, never before identified or seen in humans. It is probably safe to say that most people did not understand or even know much about viruses before the outbreak of SARS-CoV-2, which was first reported by WHO in early January 2019. According to the organization, "a cluster of cases of pneumonia of unknown cause" had been reported in the city of Wuhan, in the People's Republic of China. Chinese authorities had determined that the outbreak was caused by a novel coronavirus. Older generations in the United States and around the world may have thought back to a similar incident in world history: the 1918 influenza pandemic, a global outbreak of disease first identified in the United States in the spring of 1918.

Perhaps most people thought that thanks to modern medicine, global pandemics were a thing of the past, although most experts knew they are always a threat. Regardless, it is unlikely that anyone could have been prepared for the role politics played in the response to the pandemic, particularly in the United States.

Whatever one thought in the early days of COVID surely has changed over the course of the pandemic. Using politics and science is an interesting way to continue learning about this new disease and the potential for future pandemics. It is worth first questioning if the United States was even prepared for a pandemic. Some maintain that the US was well prepared, while others would argue otherwise. On the night of February 26, 2020, President Donald Trump shared with Americans information published in a study by the Johns Hopkins Center for Health Security. According to the center, the US ranked "number one most prepared" out of the group of 195 other world countries surveyed. Medical personnel, Americans that have lost loved ones in the pandemic, and a variety of other individuals would most likely question Trump's proclamation since the US experienced an astonishing death toll of over 600,000 within a year and a half. Why had so many died if the US ranked so high on the preparedness scale?

A pertinent question on the minds of some might reference the emergency plan prepared and published by the previous administration. According to PBS, numerous officials working for the Obama administration formulated a document detailing specific scenarios and possible actions to take under an attack of an emerging infectious disease, including pathogens described as "novel coronaviruses." What happened to the plan? Did the Trump administration put its ideas into action? These are two particularly good questions that have curiously different answers according to whom is asked. Political affiliation appears to matter. Top Republicans have said that there was no playbook. Many

Democrats, especially the ones who worked on the plan during the Obama administration, beg to differ.

Would the outcome of the pandemic have been different if another administration had been in charge? What if science and politics were not at odds with one another? What if politicians and scientific experts trusted each other and worked seamlessly together? What if medical treatment would have been available and of equal value to everyone who got sick? It seems that science and politics have been at odds for some time. The pandemic seemingly increased feelings of mistrust or dismissiveness that some individuals have for scientific or medical experts. Unquestionably, political affiliation had a big impact. Early in the pandemic, about six out of ten Democratic or Democratic-leaning independents said the coronavirus was a major threat to US health, according to Pew Research. Compare that to Republican-identifying individuals, only about three in ten of whom viewed the virus in the same way.

These statistics are not surprising considering that many Republicans and Republican-leaning voters chose to believe what President Trump said about the virus. In late February 2020, Trump began accusing Democrats of politicizing the virus, calling it "their new hoax." Again and again, Trump downplayed the virus or said that America was well prepared and that COVID was no more serious than the seasonal flu. He dismissed the advice of his medical advisers. He suggested that the severity of the global pandemic happened because the press was in a mode of hysteria. He even accused doctors and hospitals of overreporting the number of people who had died from COVID. Despite CDC recommendations, he said wearing a mask was not for him.

The results were startling. According to a Pew Research poll, about 66 percent of Republican and Republican-leaning adults said that COVID was made out to be a bigger deal than it was. Infection spread across the United States, many fell ill and died, communities quarantined, and schools and businesses shut down. And later on, Trump came down with COVID himself, was hospitalized, and recovered.

Through all the chaos, uncertainty, grief, and sadness, some things flourished.

Conspiracy theories and theorists stormed social media and their communities with questionable protests fueled by a new phenomenon. WHO even coined a term for it—the "infodemic," a term to mean the spread of false information about COVID-19. The divide between people widened, and it seemed like many could not speak to one another, even friends and families, much less use common sense. Confusing and conflicting information flooded communication venues of all kinds, and people complained they didn't know whom to listen to or believe. Let us not forget that this coronavirus and the disease it caused was a totally new infectious entity. Consequently, new health information coming out later in the pandemic occurred because experts learned about the virus and replaced earlier information with newly discovered correct guidance.

With the pandemic appearing to be almost controlled but not over, questions remain. Can the inequities of health coverage that became glaringly apparent during the pandemic be rectified? As experts agree that it's not a matter of if but when, can the United States and the world better prepare for the next pandemic? Will politicians, medical experts, and scientists gain trust of each other and the systems they work for and under? Society cannot despair. We must all continue to do our individual best so that we can strive to be better prepared for the next health crisis.

The current debate surrounding this timely topic can be understood by reading and contemplating the diverse viewpoints contained in *Current Controversies: The Politics and Science of COVID-19,* which sheds light on this ongoing contemporary issue.

CHAPTER 1

Was the United States Prepared for a Pandemic?

Overview: Could the US Have Been Better Prepared for the COVID-19 Pandemic?

Wayne Lewis

Wayne Lewis has contributed to USC Dornsife Magazine, *a publication associated with the University of Southern California.*

As the spread of COVID-19 disrupts life in many areas of the United States, the question comes to mind: Why weren't we better prepared for this?

It turns out that the very idea of a broad public health effort preparing for never-before-seen illnesses is a recent one—dating back only about 20 years.

"It's been a challenge ever since then to get political authorities, and even some public health authorities, to take pandemic preparedness seriously," says USC Dornsife College of Letters, Arts and Sciences sociologist Andrew Lakoff, the author of *Unprepared: Global Health in the Time of Emergency* (University of California Press, 2017). "It's asking people to put resources into addressing a potential threat whose probability is impossible to calculate, so attention to it has waxed and waned."

Lakoff, professor of sociology, notes that preparing for newly emerging diseases presents a host of problems that can undermine the most conscientious efforts. Nonetheless, some clear missteps have hindered our ability to lessen the spread and severity of COVID-19 in the US. What's ahead is fairly typical for outbreaks of a novel pathogen: a period of uncertainty as details about the coronavirus unspool in real time.

Why Swine Flu and Ebola Were Less Devastating

There are distinct differences between the current pandemic and the two most recent disease outbreaks, which Lakoff has studied.

"Disaster Response Expert Explains Why the US Wasn't More Prepared for the Pandemic," by Wayne Lewis, *USC Dornsife Magazine*, March 24, 2020. Reprinted by permission.

The 2009 H1N1, or swine flu, pandemic was caused by a type of influenza virus, so scientists already knew how to make a vaccine for it. By contrast, there is no vaccine for the coronavirus, which is new to humans and also more deadly than the swine flu.

On the other hand, the Ebola virus has a much higher mortality rate than the coronavirus but is far less transmissible. Although the 2014 outbreak in West Africa was catastrophic in the region, it never turned into a pandemic thanks in part to a major—if belated—global reaction, but also because the Ebola virus is more easily containable than either influenza or coronavirus.

Today, news headlines tell of the ongoing fallout from the failure to produce tests for the novel coronavirus ahead of its arrival in the US, as well as the overall lack of coordination in the federal response. Lakoff pinpoints one of the causes of this slow response as skepticism about the guidance of experts, such as scientists at the National Institute of Allergy and Infectious Diseases and the Centers for Disease Control and Prevention.

"The actual government experts in infectious disease have been on top of what's happening, but they had trouble getting their voices heard by the political folks above them," he says.

The void of clear direction from the federal government unfortunately worsens a structural quirk of US public health.

"We have a very federated system in which local and state public health agencies are fairly autonomous," says Lakoff, who also serves as divisional dean for social sciences at USC Dornsife. "They get guidelines from the CDC, but if these are not clear and coherent, you wind up with a patchwork of responses around the country."

As a result, COVID-19 in the US has turned into a sort of public health experiment, with unknown results. Over the next few months, we'll see how areas that instituted proactive responses, strictly requiring social distancing for example, fare in comparison to the many states and localities that responded slowly due to doubts about the severity of the disease.

Government Response, and Experience, Matter

There's already evidence that governmental response makes a substantial difference in mitigating COVID-19. Widespread illness and the overwhelmed health system in Italy can be partially attributed to the lack of timely, intensive measures there. Meanwhile, Taiwan and Singapore seem to have curtailed the spread and severity of the disease. Although they share certain things in common beyond geography—small size and strong central governments and public health systems—experience also likely was a factor in their favor.

Lakoff suggests that governments' experience with another member of the coronavirus family, the 2003 SARS outbreak, hastened their response to COVID-19.

"A number of observers have noted that places in East Asia were affected by SARS," Lakoff says. "The fact that SARS had directly impacted that region arguably made these governments more attentive to the possibility of a new emerging disease outbreak."

The US actually was relatively well-prepared for some disease scenarios. COVID-19 just happened not to be one of them. Fears of bioterrorism stoked by 9/11 led to a federal response that produced a substantial stockpile of botulism antitoxin and vaccines for anthrax and smallpox.

Ironic, perhaps. But nobody has a crystal ball.

"One of the paradoxes of preparedness is that you have to constantly prepare for something that might or might not happen, and you might well prepare for the wrong thing," Lakoff says. "It's highly likely that you won't be ready for what actually unfolds."

Experts Take a Cold War Approach to Preparedness

One of the main ways that policymakers and public health officials prepare for the unknown is scenario-based planning—"tabletop exercises" analyzing what could occur given a certain set of assumptions. This technique was originally developed during the Cold War to plan for a Soviet nuclear attack, and was adapted to disease preparedness in the early 2000s. Through such efforts, planners have gamed out circumstances even more dire than the current predicament—think a disease as deadly as Ebola but as easily transmitted as the flu.

However, the lessons one learns from these exercises depend upon the assumptions that are built into them.

"You only know which vulnerabilities to mitigate based on whether you appropriately planned the scenario," Lakoff says, "but it's pretty hard to do that accurately given the uncertainties involved."

Not only that, but once vulnerabilities are identified, it requires political will to dedicate the resources necessary to address them.

Uncertainty will be the status quo for the time being, even as scientists work diligently to understand and ultimately stifle the novel coronavirus. There are a number of things we won't know until after they've occurred. For example, it could take several months to understand what the actual case fatality ratio is, given the difficulty of testing across the population.

"We have to learn about the disease on the fly and figure out what works to mitigate it as quickly as possible," Lakoff says. "To do that we really depend on governments being competent, coordinated and capable of rapid and intensive intervention. As we're seeing, that's only true in certain parts of the world."

A "Pandemic Playbook" Prepared
by the Previous Administration
Was Available to Consult

Victoria Knight

Victoria Knight is a reporter with Kaiser Health News (KHN). Knight is trained in microbiology and health journalism, and her stories have appeared in several news media.

Senate Majority Leader Mitch McConnell alleged that the Obama administration did not provide the Trump administration with any information about the threat of a possible pandemic during a May 11 Team Trump Facebook Live discussion with Lara Trump.

"They claim pandemics only happen once every 100 years, but what if that is no longer true? We want to be ready, early, for the next one. Because clearly, the Obama administration did not leave any kind of game plan for something like this," said McConnell.

This claim caught our attention because its definitive nature was directly at odds with the position of some former Obama administration officials, who immediately disputed it and started circulating on social media the link to such a plan.

We reached out to McConnell's press team to ask for the basis of his statement. McConnell spokesperson David Popp said in an emailed response that "this is a unique crisis and we are all adapting to the public health and economic challenges." In terms of the pandemic's economic impact, he said there was "definitely no playbook there" and instead credited McConnell with his work on the CARES Act, a coronavirus relief bill passed by Congress.

The Pandemic Playbook

Soon after McConnell made his playbook comment, Ronald Klain, the White House Ebola response coordinator from October 2014 to

"Evidence Shows Obama Team Left a Pandemic 'Game Plan' for Trump Administration," by Victoria Knight, KHN and PolitiFact Health Check, May 15, 2020. Reprinted by permission.

February 2015, tweeted out a link to a document titled "Playbook for Early Response to High-Consequence Emerging Infectious Disease Threats and Biological Incidents."

The document, originally unearthed in March by Politico, is a 69-page National Security Council guidebook developed in 2016 with the goal of assisting leaders "in coordinating a complex US Government response to a high-consequence emerging disease threat anywhere in the world." It outlined questions to ask, who should be asked to get the answers and what key decisions should be made.

Nicole Lurie, another Obama administration official, confirmed to us the existence of the NSC pandemic playbook and also said similar documents were created for the Department of Health and Human Services and the Centers for Disease Control and Prevention.

"To say there was no playbook was ridiculous," said Lurie, who served as the assistant secretary for preparedness and response at HHS during both terms of the Obama administration.

The playbook lists types of infectious disease threats that could emerge. "Novel coronaviruses" were among pathogens flagged as having potential to cause heightened concern.

Lurie said there were tabletop exercises, which included planning for a pandemic-like situation, during the transition between the Obama and Trump administrations. (The Trump administration also conducted an exercise—known as "Crimson Contagion"—in 2019.)

Other Obama-era officials offered similar stories in interviews this week with CNN:

"They were extensively briefed, to the extent that they paid attention to these things during the transition," said Jeremy Konyndyk, who directed USAID's Office of US Foreign Disaster Assistance.

"We absolutely did leave a plan. It was called a playbook," said Lisa Monaco, former homeland security adviser to President Obama. The goal, she said, was to share the lessons learned during the Ebola and Zika outbreaks.

Meanwhile, Peter Loge, who served as a senior adviser within Obama's Food and Drug Administration, told KHN he remembered a very clear message from the HHS secretary regarding the presidential transition.

"Our job was to set up the Trump political staff for success, and we took that mandate very seriously," said Loge. He and his colleagues wrote memos to inform the Trump staff about priority issues. "But nobody called me and asked what I was doing in my job," said Loge.

However, the Trump administration has maintained that the coronavirus sneaked up on the US, and Trump himself has even said it was a "very unforeseen thing."

But, in a May 14 exchange with reporters on the White House lawn, press secretary Kayleigh McEnany acknowledged the existence of the Obama pandemic playbook, even holding it up to show the press. She also dismissed its usefulness.

"The Obama-Biden plan that has been referenced was insufficient. It wasn't going to work. What our administration did under the leadership of President Trump was do an entire 2018 pandemic preparedness report," said McEnany. Trump, who was standing nearby, agreed.

Our Ruling

Senate Majority Leader Mitch McConnell said the Obama administration did not leave behind a "game plan" for a pandemic.

That's wrong.

Multiple Obama-era officials have said they left a 2016 "pandemic playbook" that detailed exact steps to take in the event of an infectious disease outbreak. The White House press secretary even held up the actual document on the White House lawn.

There has been discussion in recent days as to whether the Obama plan was dated because it dealt with lessons learned from earlier outbreaks that may not apply to the current pandemic. Still, McConnell's statement focused only on whether any such "game plan" existed, and ample evidence suggests it did.

We rate it Pants on Fire.

UPDATE, May 15, 2020, 11:04 am ET: In a Fox News interview, McConnell acknowledged he was incorrect in his assertion that the Obama administration didn't leave behind any kind of "game plan" regarding a pandemic threat. "I was wrong. They did leave behind a plan, so I clearly made a mistake in that regard," McConnell said.

US Schools Quickly Pivoted to Online Learning During Lockdown

Anya Kamenetz

Since 2014, Anya Kamenetz has been an education correspondent at NPR. She has authored several books, the latest being The Art of Screen Time: How Your Family Can Balance Digital Media and Real Life.

For 6-year-old Sadie Hernandez, the first day of online school started at her round, wooden kitchen table in Jacksonville, Fla. She turned on an iPad and started talking to her first grade teacher, Robin Nelson.

"Are you ready to do this online stuff?" her teacher asks, in a video sent to NPR by Hernandez's mother, Audrey.

"Yeah," Sadie responds.

"It's kind of scary isn't it?"

"Kind of."

Sadie's teacher reminds her that they'll be using the educational software that she is already familiar with from her face-to-face classes at Ortega Elementary School: "It's iReady, so we've got that. And we've got WritingCity. And now you know how to meet me in the morning."

Every state has closed at least some public schools to fight the spread of coronavirus, and some are starting to say they expect to be closed through the end of the school year.

Thrown into the breach, public schools are setting out on an unprecedented experiment: With little training and even fewer resources, in a matter of days they're shifting from a system of education that for centuries has focused on face to face interaction, to one that works entirely at a distance.

Diana Greene, the superintendent of Duval County Schools where Robin Nelson teaches, sent an email to her staff on Friday, March 20 that illustrates the magnitude of the effort educators around the country are faced with:

"It is amazing to me that it was just 3 days ago that we made the decision to close schools. In less than 72 hours, Team Duval moved the entire district to an at-home, virtual instruction model. We have managed to troubleshoot the mobilization of meal programs, lack of technology equipment, online teacher training, and a whole host of issues that come with a change of this magnitude. Three days!

"Three days to create, print and distribute about 5 million pages of instructional content. Three days to load classes onto an online platform. Three days to gather online resources so aligned instruction could continue to take place. Three days to train about 8,000 teachers in a whole new way of work. Imagine that!

"Three days to conduct a survey of technology needs from 130,000 students and to prepare thousands of computers for student use. Three days to prepare for neighborhood delivery of school lunches and snacks on our buses so children would not go hungry. Just three days to mobilize a community of partners and volunteers to assist our schools."

Some families, like Sadie's, are adjusting reasonably well. Her parents are both working from home, still earning paychecks. When Sadie has to concentrate on her lessons, they turn on "Daniel Tiger" for her little sister Kate. There's a backyard swimming pool for cooling off when lessons are done.

But as a crisis often does, this one has exposed existing inequalities—among schools, among districts and among students. Just over half of the nation's public school children are from families considered low-income, and an estimated 12 million lack broadband Internet access at home.

Robin Nelson, an educator with 10 years experience, says one of the students in her class has special needs and needs significant accommodation, and the family also struggles financially. "I've spoken to his mom. There's another little one on the way, if not already arrived."

And, Nelson notes, for that family and many like it, "survival is a priority and not, you know, accommodations right now for him." Nelson thinks the student may end up repeating a grade. She's also concerned about children whose parents must go out to work, and who are sending their kids to home-based daycares that remain open.

She tears up talking about her "babies" and how much she misses greeting them at the door with a fist-bump, handshake or hug. Sadie Hernandez wrote a note and drew pictures to leave on her beloved teacher's doorstep.

Because of these inherent inequities, some researchers are advocating that public schools focus on making up lost learning when things get back to normal—through summer school and other remediation. That will take extra funding, including money to pay teachers. Douglas Harris, an education researcher and fellow at the Brookings Institution, has written a post calling for school districts to focus on making up time, not on teaching remotely:

"Studies of online learning suggest not only that students learn less in online environments, compared with in person, but that disadvantaged students learn the least. And that's true even when online teachers have experience and training with online teaching. Under the current emergency, most teachers will not have any experience at all with this approach."

Nevertheless, with its latest guidance, the federal Education Department has encouraged schools closing due to coronavirus to pursue distance learning quote "creatively" and with "flexibility," even if they can't reach every student that way.

Reminding everyone that this is an unprecedented situation, "No one wants to have learning coming to a halt across America due to the COVID-19 outbreak," reads the guidance, "and the US Department of Education does not want to stand in the way of good faith efforts to educate students on-line."

The Senate coronavirus relief package passed on Wednesday includes $13.5 billion earmarked for schools, which they can use to keep paying staff as well as to buy new technology.

As they wait for clearer direction, materials, and training, states and districts are choosing different paths. In the Philadelphia area, districts may use up snow days left over from the mild winter. In Chicago, teachers are offering enrichment resources only, instructed to make sure there's "no new learning." Harking back to an earlier era of distance education, Los Angeles Unified is partnering with the local public television stations to pair educational broadcasts with some online resources.

Florida, where Robin Nelson teaches, is an example of a state that has moved swiftly to transition as much instruction as possible online. Partly that's because it is home to the Florida Virtual School. That's a public, nonprofit K12 school that has been around for over two decades, and has a solid reputation—its students do about as well as, or a little better than, other students in the state.

Before the outbreak, FLVS directly enrolled 200,000 students, primarily in Florida but also across all 50 states and overseas. Now they are looking to double that direct enrollment by the end of April. And the school is also training at least 10,000 Florida teachers to transition their own classes online—via live online trainings and pre-recorded webinars.

"We've partnered with the [state] Department of Education to work with the school districts to support teacher professional development at the district level, to help them ramp up and to be able to teach students online," says Courtney Calfee, executive director for global services at FLVS.

Nelson says she and other teachers at Ortega Elementary cobbled together online lessons from various sources: "It's teachers going through and kind of pulling out their materials, saying, hey, PBS has a good thing over here ..."

Paula Renfro leads professional development for Duval County Public Schools, the district where Nelson teaches. She says that in making this swift transition, they decided to lead with their existing "blended learning resource library," including software programs and digital textbooks.

"Really, when we considered how this rollout was going to look, we needed to provide tools, especially in the beginning, that teachers and students had a high comfort level with."

Another big consideration for schools making this transition is how much time per day to attempt to connect live with students—known as "synchronous," or real-time, learning—versus putting out assignments for students to complete on their own—known as asynchronous learning.

Where schools and communities have more resources, they seem to be gravitating more toward the synchronous model.

NPR put out a call on Twitter and Facebook, and among the responses were families with students at a dozen private schools around the country that are holding live online classes via video chat for up to five hours per day.

Interestingly, Justin Reich, an online learning researcher at MIT, says this isn't necessarily the best approach to use, especially in the younger grades. "Young people don't have the attention or the executive function skills to be able to sit and learn online for hours every day on their own."

He advocates instead a pattern sometimes known as "hybrid," "blended learning" or a "flipped classroom." It's a combination of relatively short, live video check-in meetings and self-paced work, with teachers available to students over email, phone, text or any other method that is convenient to both. In fact, if you are working remotely right now as an adult, it might look pretty similar to that.

That's more or less what Robin Nelson is doing with those of her students who are able to connect with her. They do a version of "morning meeting" using Microsoft Teams, videoconferencing every morning at 8:30. There, she gives them the assignments for the day.

After that, Nelson makes herself available for virtual "office hours" from 9 to 11 a.m., so parents can check in. Families are also contacting her throughout the day on their smartphones using ClassDojo, a program she was already using to keep in touch. She's encouraging parents to read to children every day, and even to have some kind of recess.

Florida Virtual School does something similar with what it calls its "high teacher touch" approach. Assignments are designed to be completed on students' own time. The teacher holds live lessons via video chat either weekly or daily, depending on the course, where students can also talk to each other. At FLVS, some courses also have what's called "discussion-based assessment," where the teacher has a live video conversation with the student to check for mastery.

There's one big caveat. This model, Reich says, overwhelmingly relies on a parent or caregiver who can serve as a coach, cheerleader, IT support and general troubleshooter. Until you get perhaps to late middle or high school, there is no such thing as independent solo school via computer—most students just aren't developmentally capable of it.

Most of all, Nelson is wondering why her district threw "a ton of work" into creating an online model when many of the students she calls "her babies" don't have adequate resources to connect right now.

"Some of them have laptops. Some of them have siblings that will be sharing that technology. So, you know, that will make it more difficult." Others, she says, will be using a parent's phone at best. "But if the parents are trying to work from home or whatever they're trying to do, it's not gonna be a priority."

These students who told the school they lacked connectivity, for now, are getting paper homework packets, handed out along with free food from the school lunch program. The plan is to collect the packets in two weeks. The district, like others around the country, is lending out laptops and mobile hotspot devices, but in Duval County middle and high school students get priority over the elementary school students.

For the paper packets, "Who's collecting and who's grading it? How are these kids getting feedback on what they're doing?" Nelson asks. "All that's just pretty gray right now." She said that during the first week, out of 19 students, "I have 12 that are working online for at least some (if not all) of the assignments, four that have packets only, two more that have packets but plan on picking up a computer from the district to borrow, and one student that is AWOL."

Renfro, who works for the district, notes that this is early days, and the district hopes to continue getting resources out to students who need them. For students who don't have computers yet, "we are contacting families through email, telephone each day," she says. "We still have our hands and our arms wrapped around them to support them."

Medical Professionals Shattered the Illusion That the US Was Ready for an Outbreak

Nikhila Natarajan

Nikhila Natarajan is a senior program manager for media and digital content with the Observer Research Foundation.

As the US coronavirus case load nears the 200,000 mark, the death toll inches towards the 4,000 and America braces for a worst case scenario of 200,000 deaths, doctors, nurses, frontline healthcare workers and caregivers are bubbling into our screens not merely in their work avatars but as surrogates for the anxious commoner, co-creators of medical gear and storytellers working on the cliff-edge of a pandemic.

Shaken by their own high-risk exposure to the virus, the lack of personal protective gear and incredible physical strain, this community has brought on the latest breed of digital radicals talking to us from where cameras cannot go and where people are saying their final goodbyes in utter isolation. Doctors and nurses are showing us a mirror to our interconnected vulnerabilities; they have shattered the illusion that the US was ready for this outbreak. Medical lingo is having its breakout moment. When was the last time words like "comorbidities," "immunocompromised," "viral load factor," "attack rate," and "underlying conditions" were the stuff of red hot social threads for days on end? The medical is now everyone's personal, caregivers are the rock stars of the emerging Covid 19 culture and mighty governments are bowing to their collective wisdom.

Here are three takeaways from an edgy new style of real-time public education in the annals of America's new social order:

"COVID19 in the US: Doctors as Storytellers," by Nikhila Natarajan, Observer Research Foundation, April 1, 2020. Reprinted by permission.

1. How Two Doctors Forced a Trump U-Turn

Let's start right at the top and then go downstream. Here's how US president Donald Trump, who talked up opening the US economy before Easter weekend, did a 180 degree turn within hours. The abrupt shift came after two of America's most renowned doctors—Dr. Anthony Fauci and Dr. Deborah Birx—spearheading the White House Covid 19 task force—spread out their charts on Trump's desk. "Dr. Debbie Birx and I went into the Oval Office and leaned over the desk and said, 'Here are the data, take a look.' He just shook his head and said, 'I guess we got to do it,'" Fauci explains. The charts that Fauci refers to are predictive models showing millions of deaths if there was zero mitigation in place. Of the two doctors, Birx has found ways to warn Americans about the virus in deeply personal terms.

As Americans grappled with Phase One of social distancing norms, Birx dusted out the story of her grandmother Leah who "lived with a lifetime of guilt" because she caught the flu at school and brought it home to her mother who had just given birth. Leah's mother died of the flu—one of an estimated 50 million worldwide who died in the 1918 influenza epidemic. "I can tell you, my grandmother lived with that for 88 years," Birx said, and added: "This is not a theoretic. This is a reality." Fauci, America's top infectious diseases doctor, has become a national star for his "data-led" storytelling. Raspy voiced, Fauci, who has advised every president since Ronald Reagan, is now the subject of fan art, donuts and socks which are selling out as he rocks Instagram and YouTube and linear TV all at once. Fauci's 30-minute Instagram conversation with basketball star Stephen Curry has become a yardstick for jargon-free public education. The image of the wealthy, infected celebrity is no longer the barometer for this transformational moment. In the altered universe, that frame belongs to stoic, sleepless, "mathy" kind of people in scrubs.

2. Delivering on the Original
Promise of Social Platforms

For all the flak that social media platforms got after the 2016 US elections, the Covid 19 pandemic is showing that Twitter, Facebook, YouTube and others are journeying back to their original promise of helping communities organise. Out there in the hospitals, caregivers and frontline staff have become our go-to sources for media reportage from the trenches, when they're not intubating patients or triaging.

Responsible voices are breaking through and helping the world shorten turnaround times on understanding a crisis in real time. Urgency oozes from a Stanford doctor's tweet asking for best practices for "last resort" homemade masks. "Sewing patterns? Evidence? Filter pocket? Materials?" she writes. Stumbling out of red eye shifts, medical residents are penning hurried notes to the world. "Last night in the ICU of a #NYC hospital, I cared for 20 patients who were all on breathing machines due to #COVID19. Some really young (20s), without comorbidities. Everyone is extremely sick. But sicker patients keep flooding in." While Fauci and Birx got the charts ready, doctors outside the White House kept up the pressure. Reacting with alarm to Trump's comments, America's best and brightest medical professionals pushed back on the US president's favorite platform. "If you don't solve the medical crisis, you will not solve the economic crisis. #Buyustime," Pulitzer Prize winning oncologist-writer Dr. Siddhartha Mukherjee tweeted. "The 15 day quarantine plan is a disaster," he said. Wherever state governments are keeping a safe distance from taking tough calls, doctors are wading in fearlessly. Should we all be wearing masks? While governments told us masks are not needed, practicing physicians debunked it and began requiring everyone in their hospitals to wear it, not just the first line staff. A grassroots pro-mask movement supercharged by social media educational content has already changed how people are covering their faces in America's neighborhoods.

Before this, it was school closures. There too, the "government does not recommend it" was the operative recommendation. The community took over, driven to action by the last doctor or nurse's post they saw on their phones. That distance between doctors and the masses has rarely been smaller than it is now.

3. In Doctors' Questions, We Find Our Answers

Doctors turned storytellers have taken their sophisticated writing to the masses and we are all better for it. The questions they are asking tell us how much we don't know, and we, in turn, are filling those gaps with obsessive hand washing, mask wearing and disinfecting—actions that makes us all safer. Can we quantify the increase in risk for higher exposure to the Covid 19? What about the severity of the initial exposure? How much of a role does the first hit play in how ill the patient becomes? Is there data on how the virus moves through the body? How much of the Singapore–Hong Kong policy is essential to flatten the curve elsewhere? Even as we absorb the meaning of these unknowns and evaluate our options for the micro-moments of our lives, our social media feeds turn surreal again. Take David Lat, who describes himself as an athletic 44 year old, "asleep in a normal hospital room, and the next thing I knew, I was in a scene out of *ER*—being shot up with drugs and having a tube shoved down my throat." Elsewhere, a woman from Nevada sends us a "gentle reminder to hold your loved ones tight tonight if you can" and then 10 hours later, tells of her grandmother's passing, from Covid 19. As we turn inwards and find new rituals in closed spaces, our fingers, more shriveled each day from excessive hand washing, stumble into new storytellers.

Government Failed to Keep the US Prepared for COVID

Daniel M. Gerstein

Daniel M. Gerstein is an adjunct professor at American University teaching courses on biodefense. Gerstein was acting undersecretary for science and technology at the Department of Homeland Security.

By the end of February, two months after China reported a mysterious cluster of pneumonia cases to the World Health Organization, the disease we now know as COVID-19 had already claimed almost 3,000 lives. The new coronavirus had spread to 53 countries and sickened some 85,000 people, including more than 60 people in the United States.

But despite the Trump administration implementing a partial travel ban on China on February 2, and travel restrictions on Europe shortly thereafter, the US government was not marshaling a strong response to the crisis. It was not until March 13 when President Donald Trump declared a national emergency that the government's response became fully engaged. By then, of course, the disease was already spreading throughout the country.

Early on in the outbreak, at a time when better preparations could have been made to forestall the worst impacts of a broad outbreak, the federal response was failing. To paraphrase a former senior emergency management official in Chicago, the cavalry was not coming. Biosurveillance data on the scope of the outbreak wasn't being heeded. Disease tests and vital medical equipment were not being supplied. The network of officials and offices related to emergency management that had trained together on how to respond to a pandemic had been superseded by an ad hoc White House task force.

"Epic Fail: Why the US Wasn't Prepared for the Coronavirus Pandemic," by Daniel M. Gerstein, *Bulletin of the Atomic Scientists*, April 24, 2020. This April 2020 article originally appeared in the *Bulletin of the Atomic Scientists* and has been reprinted with permission.

Understanding the shortfalls in the federal role to date will be essential in mitigating the effects of, responding to, and recovering from COVID-19, as well as better preparing for future events. There are at least three important areas where the federal government hasn't played the role it should have.

Inadequate Biosurveillance

The roots of why the federal response has been so halting during the first few months of the COVID-19 pandemic can be traced back two decades, to a prior era when US officials were becoming acutely aware of the potential for a major biological incident.

The 9/11 terrorist attacks were the last events to expose a national vulnerability even remotely comparable to the COVID-19 pandemic. Shortly after the attacks, a scientist working at an Army disease research lab added to the unease that had settled on the country by allegedly sending out letters filled with deadly anthrax spores to politicians and media figures. The so-called Amerithrax attacks sickened 17 and killed five, providing a case study for why officials needed to bolster national biodefense.

During the post-9/11 era, officials gave particular attention to improving the country's capabilities in biosurveillance, defined by the White House as "active data-gathering with appropriate analysis and interpretation of biosphere data that might relate to disease activity and threats to human or animal health." Government offices undertook myriad activities in the name of biosurveillance. Strategies were written. Training was conducted and exercises were held. Offices like the National Biosurveillance Integration Center were created to integrate "information from thousands of sources about biological threats" to improve "early warning and situational awareness."

At the end of the day, biosurveillance comes down to having the capacity to sense that a disease is present, so actions can be taken to halt its spread. It comes down to using testing and diagnostics to determine who is and who has been infected, conducting contact tracing to identify who might have been exposed so they can take mitigation protocols, and sharing information, so public health officials can understand how the disease has or has not been controlled. Armed with this biosurveillance data, public health professionals can make data-informed recommendations, and leaders can take action.

In the years following 9/11, biosurveillance systems and plans were put in place to provide the government an opportunity to watch for and react to something like a pandemic virus. But despite strong pronouncements and good intentions, funding shortfalls, organizational disfunction, and problems with information sharing have long confounded federal efforts. By the time COVID-19 first appeared, three different presidential administrations had struggled to develop an effective national biosurveillance system.

All this is not to say that parts of the US government, such as the Centers for Disease Control and Prevention (CDC) and the National Center for Medical Intelligence within the intelligence community, aren't tasked with biosurveillance responsibilities, but rather that, overall, it's difficult to argue that the biosurveillance system operates like a well-oiled machine. Both organizations have raised concerns about COVID-19 since early January; however, these admonitions were largely unheeded by the administration until mid-March.

Failures in developing a timely testing protocol for diagnosing the disease contributed to biosurveillance shortfalls and the ineffective national response to COVID-19. The test for the coronavirus developed by the CDC was not accurate and had to be recalled, causing important delays in understanding the spread of the disease in the United States. Even now, the rate of testing lags behind requirements, and there are not enough tests to go around, a major problem for states as they begin to consider lifting stay-at-home orders and easing social distancing restrictions.

A Disrupted Emergency Response Network

After 9/11, government officials aggressively developed a so-called national exercise program designed to bring key stakeholders together to force them to confront various scenario-based national emergencies, from hurricanes and tornados to cyberattacks and pandemics. The exercises are intended to test preparedness and response systems as well as support functions and communications chains. The scenario-based exercises are designed to place the actual decisionmakers and specialists throughout the government in difficult and complex positions that require them to react to constantly changing inputs and new information. When the president stood up the coronavirus task force at the end of January and subsequently replaced Secretary of Health and Human Services Alex Azar as its head, officials across the government found themselves dealing with a different system than the one they had trained on.

Ironically, standing up the task force, which was intended to organize the federal fight against COVID-19, disconnected some of the relationships that were important for conducting a coherent emergency response. Many of those relationships ran down from Azar's office and into state public health offices that were in charge of their states' responses. Emergency management personnel in state and local offices found it harder to make decisions on how to respond to the crisis. Normal chains for distributing information or supplies didn't work as well. Unfortunately, not relying on established emergency-management doctrine at the federal level has exacerbated the confusion at the state and local level as well.

By the end of February, Trump replaced Azar and put Vice President Mike Pence at the helm of the coronavirus task force, a role in which Pence has basically been getting high marks as a stabilizing influence. Nonetheless, when the administration or the president shuffles the deck and as officials fall in and out of favor, there can be real-world implications.

Supply Chain (Mis)Management

State governments across the country are finding they are in a competition with other states and the federal government over medical supplies. They're being left to fend for themselves, and the federal government isn't taking control of the supply chain to efficiently distribute resources.

The pandemic is highlighting the need to rethink how supplies are stored and distributed in an emergency. In particular, it's casting a harsh spotlight on the Strategic National Stockpile. Originally created in 1998, the stockpile of emergency supplies and medications is maintained by the assistant secretary for preparedness and response within the Department of Health and Human Services. While the stockpile was designed to provide support during a pandemic response, the level at which it was provisioned and the types of vaccines and therapeutics it contained indicate there was a predisposition to preparing for a bioterrorism event or a much smaller public health emergency, such as the 2014 Ebola response.

General equipment in the stockpile such as personal protective equipment and ventilators would be useful in either a pandemic or bioterrorism event, but the stockpile was not envisioned to have enough for supplying a national crisis of this magnitude. The stockpile just doesn't have the amounts of the supplies governors say they need to fight COVID-19. That's a big part of the reason many states have been left to scour the open market. The Trump administration meanwhile, changed its definition of the stockpile's purpose midway through the pandemic, contextualizing it more as a "stopgap" than a primary resource for states to use.

A Make-Over for Emergency Response

Trump's direction to governors to "step up efforts to get medical supplies" overturned preparedness and response procedures that have evolved since the Congressional Act of 1803, which provided federal assistance to a New Hampshire town following a fire.

Much of the way the United States thought about emergency management before the current pandemic traces directly back to this history. Emergency management in the United States is based on the understanding that all initial response is local. When local authorities no longer have the capacity to mount an effective response, states provide necessary support. When the state capacity is exhausted, the president can make what's called a Stafford Act declaration and provide federal support for disaster relief.

Two hundred-plus years of thinking and practice in the field of emergency management have produced a system that imagines a strong federal response to disasters. Now, US emergency management experience seems to be getting a make-over. Following months of criticizing the support they've been receiving from the federal government, state governments have begun to form pacts to coordinate their response to the outbreak and sometimes even to bypass the federal government.

Despite three successive presidential administrations that placed substantial emphasis on biodefense, the COVID-19 crisis has exposed underlying cracks in the national preparedness and response system. Going forward, the United States will need to question and in some cases relearn the lessons of crisis response and emergency management. Undoubtedly, national funding will need to be reconsidered to ensure that crisis response budgets are aligned with American priorities. Just as in the aftermath of other response failures in US history—Hurricane Katrina and the terrorist attacks of 9/11 come to mind—a public reckoning needs to occur, if the failures of the federal government are to be well-enough understood to reduce the probability that they will recur.

PPE Shortages Revealed the US Government's Lack of Preparedness

Tucker Doherty and Brianna Ehley

Tucker Doherty and Brianna Ehley are both health reporters for Politico.

President Donald Trump often opens his evening news briefings on the pandemic by rattling off a list of actions his administration has taken to secure protective gear for frontline health workers, claiming dire shortages have been resolved.

But hospitals, nursing homes and caregivers across the country tell Politico they are still struggling to obtain medical masks, gloves and gowns, undercutting Trump's assertions.

For this story, reporters in the past week spoke with 17 health care workers and officials across the country, including some who responded to a Politico survey about working conditions on the front lines of coronavirus. Some spoke on condition of anonymity because they feared retribution, because some hospitals have threatened to fire workers for airing their concerns publicly.

The interviews reveal a medical workforce still struggling to adapt to dangerous conditions with little confidence that the available protective gear is being steered to the places it's needed most. Some say they're still being forced to reuse masks or MacGyver their own equipment four months into the US outbreak, even as Trump dismisses questions about shortages as "fake news," as he did earlier this month.

"We had very little in our stockpile," Trump said in a recent briefing. "Now we're loaded up. And we also loaded up these hospitals."

"Trump Called PPE Shortages 'Fake News.' Health Care Workers Say They're Still a Real Problem," by Tucker Doherty and Brianna Ehley, Politico, April 26, 2020. Reprinted by permission.

Without a more robust supply of personal protective equipment, or PPE, the fast-moving virus will continue to pose an unprecedented threat to America's health care workforce, having already sickened at least 9,282 medical workers and killed 27. Those grim numbers, which come from a CDC report almost two weeks ago, are certainly an undercount.

And enduring shortages of protective gear could also set back timelines for reopening parts of the country and make it more difficult for cash-starved hospitals to resume elective procedures. Trump's own guidelines say states should have adequate supplies of protective and medical equipment before dialing back social distancing restrictions.

States and hospitals say they have faced unusual challenges in their scramble to secure PPE—from a strained global supply chain and the Trump administration itself. They complain Trump's encouragement of states to hunt down supplies on their own has created a chaotic competition for PPE and medical equipment. In some cases, states have accused the federal government of seizing shipments of protective equipment to distribute to another region, though the Federal Emergency Management Agency has denied those claims.

In interviews, doctors and nurses described restrictive hospital policies limiting workers to a single mask per day, though the equipment is supposed to be discarded after a single use to lower the risk of spreading infection. Others said workplace guidelines aimed at conserving gear are constantly shifting with little explanation of why. They described hospital administrators keeping unusually close tabs on their supply, and workers report being reprimanded for using basic protective gear outside of units designated for coronavirus patients.

"There's no way that anyone could possibly think that what is happening now is acceptable, even in its improved form. It's still not enough," said a hospital physician in Georgia who requested anonymity. "To feel that you can't do your job without begging, especially if you're putting your body on the line, that you can't get the tools you need without being gaslighted or interrogated, there's something belittling and patronizing about it."

Because of supply shortages, she said nurses at the safety-net Atlanta hospital where she works have wrapped stethoscopes in medical gloves to reuse them on multiple coronavirus patients, instead of following the recommended practice of using a dedicated disposable stethoscope for each patient. While mask supplies have improved, some doctors who worry about future shortages are keeping backup stashes in brown paper bags, she said.

Surveys of health care workers across the country appear to echo their concerns. A majority of those treating Covid-19 patients said they were worried about shortages of a vast array of protective equipment, including isolation gowns, N-95 masks and face shields, according to a poll earlier this month from the health services firm Premier. Additionally, 70 percent said providers were reusing masks to save supplies.

There are some small signs of improvement, however. While most critical care physicians in California said they were worried about protective equipment shortages, the most extreme concerns have faded since early April, according to a survey by the California Health Care Foundation.

A spokesperson for FEMA, which is overseeing the federal government's distribution of supplies, said the agency has received "a number of requests for assistance from states and localities to fill PPE shortages." The Trump administration, as it works across the government and with industry to locate more PPE, has already sent out 66.9 million N-95 respirator masks, 105 million surgical masks and roughly 14 million gowns, the spokesperson said.

Still, states and health workers say they need more to fight a stealthy and highly contagious disease that Trump's health experts believe will still be here in the fall.

Groups representing long-term care facilities including nursing homes say they still haven't been prioritized for PPE, even though the virus has ravaged their high-risk populations. Thousands of deaths in long-term care facilities have been linked to the coronavirus, and more than 650 facilities have reported cases.

The American Health Care Association, the national group for long-term care providers, said three-quarters of its members are running out of PPE, and about 60 percent are reusing or improvising PPE.

"We have shortages in all categories of PPE," said Tony Marshall, president and CEO of the group's Georgia chapter. Marshall said workers in some facilities have been wearing homemade masks and raincoats for gowns because of struggles procuring medical equipment.

Health workers who visit patients in their homes say they are making the rounds while facing many of the same equipment shortages. Service Employees International Union regional president Sterling Harders, whose chapter represents more than 45,000 nursing home, home care and residential care workers throughout Washington state and Montana, said the union is pushing for more protective gear.

"The fact of the matter is, many caregivers don't have masks as of today, and we're not gonna rest until all those who need masks have them," said Harders.

A nurse in Montana said while her hospital has so far weathered the crisis, officials are scrambling to locate PPE because they fear being unprepared if a larger wave hits the state.

"They set up a situation where states are bidding against each other," she said. "We're a poor state."

The White House Disregarded Its Own Pandemic Experts

Ana Maria Lankford, Derrick Storzieri, and Joseph Fitsanakis

Ana Maria Lankford is in the Department of Politics at Coastal Carolina University. Derrick Storzieri headed the North America Desk of the Chanticleer Intelligence Brief in the Intelligence and National Security Studies program at Coastal Carolina University. Joseph Fitsanakis is associate professor of politics in the Intelligence and National Security Studies program at Coastal Carolina University.

From the very onset of SARS-CoV-2 (also known as the novel coronavirus), United States President Donald Trump has led his senior administration officials in a chorus of statements claiming that the pandemic "came out of nowhere" (Trump, 2020a) and that "nobody saw it coming" (Trump, 2020b). The US President has repeatedly described the virus as an "invisible enemy," which "snuck up on us" and which "nobody could have predicted" (Bump, 2020). Such statements have no basis in fact. A growing body of evidence demonstrates that the US Intelligence Community (IC) has been repeatedly warning policy- and decision-makers for well over a decade about the potentially catastrophic effects of highly infectious respiratory viruses. In numerous reports, which date to at least 2004, the IC has cautioned US decision-makers of the impending human security threat of a global health pandemic. In these reports, IC analysts use stark language to warn that the United States lacks the capacity to contain a fast-spreading disease and stabilize the economy amidst an impending—not a possible—health pandemic (Miller P., 2020).

"Spies and the Virus: The COVID-19 Pandemic and Intelligence Communication in the United States," by Ana Maria Lankford, Derrick Storzieri, and Joseph Fitsanakis, *Frontiers in Communication*, December 3, 2020. https://www.frontiersin.org/articles/10.3389/fcomm.2020.582245/full. Licensed under CC BY-4.0 International.

The Trump administration's emphasis on the alleged lack of forewarning is likely part of a political strategy designed to shield the president and other senior officials from mounting criticism over the federal government's slow response to the novel coronavirus outbreak. The administration did not begin taking moderate steps toward a nationwide response to the virus until 16 March, several weeks after leading epidemiologists began calling for the imposition of aggressive measures to combat the disease. The dramatic impact of the absence of early containment and mitigation in the US can be observed in a comparative data assessment of the US and two other leading industrialized countries, Japan and South Korea. On February 29, 2020, Japan (population 126 million) had recorded five deaths due to COVID-19—the disease caused by the novel coronavirus. On the same day, South Korea (population 51 million) had recorded 17 novel coronavirus-related deaths, while the US (population 328 million) had recorded a single death from the disease. By 5 July, Japan had recorded 977 deaths from COVID-19, which equated to 7.7 deaths per million people. South Korea had recorded 283 deaths, which equated to 5.5 deaths per million people. The United States had reached 132,318 deaths, or 403 deaths per million people (Johns Hopkins University, 2020). Epidemiological models produced in recent months show that "an estimated 90 percent of the cumulative deaths in the United States from COVID-19 [...] might have been prevented by putting social distancing policies into effect 2 weeks earlier, on March 2" (Jewell and Jewell, 2020). As research from Columbia University shows, even if such measures had been put in place only a week earlier, on 9 March, the US could have seen "~60 percent reduction in deaths" nationwide (Kandula and Shaman, 2020).

[...]

Biosurveillance and Disease Intelligence Functions of the US Government

In addition to posing major challenges in the areas of healthcare and public health, disease outbreaks can test the limits of national security doctrines. At the pandemic level, such outbreaks—whether naturally occurring or bioengineered—can quickly and irreversibly degrade complex economic systems by severing their production and distribution functions, and even severing demand for goods and services. In the words of former US Director of National Intelligence Dan Coats, disease outbreaks can lead to "major economic and societal disruptions" (Office of the Director of National Intelligence, 2018a), which, if left unchecked, can deliver mortal blows to the stability of states. It follows that the monitoring of disease outbreaks falls within the operational scope of the US IC, an amalgamation of 17 organizations, whose mission is to gather, analyze and disseminate intelligence to American policy- and decision-makers. Consumers of intelligence products use them to inform their judgment in the course of pursuing sound and effective governance.

In the US, federal biosurveillance and biodefense tasks are diffused within an extremely wide spectrum, which is known as the US Biological Defense Program. It includes analytical units, such as the Department of Homeland Security's Chemical and Biological Defense Division. It also encompasses protection units, such as the Office of Preparedness and Response of the Department of Health and Human Services (DHHS). Importantly for this paper, it also features units that combine intelligence collection and analysis tasks, such as the Disease Intelligence Program of the Central Intelligence Agency's (CIA) Directorate of Science and Technology. The latter constitutes one of the earliest components of the US Biological Defense Program, with roots that date to the 1966 cerebrospinal meningitis outbreak in Beijing, China (Kawai, 2014). The outbreak prompted the Chinese government to shut down schools and implement a military takeover of the healthcare system. This prompted the CIA's Office of Scientific Intelligence to launch Project IMPACT, an effort to aggregate disease data in order to assess the political fallout of the disease (Carey and Maxfield, 1972). In 1968, when the Hong Kong/A2/68 influenza killed an estimated 4 million people, including around 100,000 Americans (Vuboud et al., 2005), Project IMPACT was merged with a grander effort, codenamed Project BLACKFLAG. Its goal was to "computerize disease information and derive trends, cycles and predictions" (Ferran, 2020) on a global scale. Through BLACKFLAG, the CIA was also able to warn its teams of operatives abroad, instructing them to shield themselves from the flu as it spread in East Asia and, eventually, the world (Ferran, 2020).

The CIA's early disease intelligence efforts showed that data aggregation was critical in helping monitor and forecast outbreaks at a quick pace. They also demonstrated the direct integration of such data with political, military and economic intelligence. Finally, they helped shape the 3-fold mission of disease intelligence, which remains fundamentally unchanged to this day, and is as follows: (a) collect intelligence about the extent and spread of diseases abroad, which may vary widely from data provided by official state sources; (b) forecast the consequences of these trends for American interests in the affected regions; and (c) provide policy- and decision-makers with the information they need to protect American lives and property from the effects of diseases. Since 1966, disease intelligence data have been disseminated to American decision-and policy-makers in a variety of formats and without interruption.

It is important to call attention to the fact that the mandate of the US IC does not include making policy decisions. These are left to elected or appointed decision-makers in the civilian and military realms. Thus, the role of intelligence analysts in the US Biological Defense Program ends once they disseminate the information that has been collected, analyzed and incorporated into finished intelligence products. Dissemination—i.e., the communication of finished intelligence products to the consumer—is a distinct phase of what is known as "the intelligence cycle"—a term that refers to the process that intelligence professionals utilize in order to effectively analyze and communicate information collected in the field. Conceptual models of the intelligence cycle differ, but most versions consist of five phases: planning and direction;

collection; processing; analysis and production; and dissemination [Johnston, 2005]. These steps are interchangeable, allowing for intelligence practitioners to begin at any phase of the intelligence cycle, or to revert to previous phases, in order to create effective intelligence products.

The intelligence cycle typically begins when an intelligence agency assigns tasks to its employees to carry out. This can be an independent action by an agency, or can result once it is tasked by decision-makers—referred to as "customers"—with providing a deliverable, whether that be information, or a physical piece of evidence that could be analyzed to produce effective, actionable intelligence. This process is referred to as Planning and Direction. The completion of this stage leads to the collection of raw data. Collection can be categorized as open-source, clandestine, and covert. Open-source collection utilizes unrestricted networks and officially released documents to obtain information. Clandestine collection involves engagement into secret collection efforts, which is broadly acknowledged by governments—since most governments generally admit to maintaining clandestine collection capabilities. This could involve the use of field agents in the form of diplomats or assets (spies) to collect data. Covert collection involves actions that are tasked by the government, but not sanctioned, so as to avert escalating conflict between nations if collection operations are detected. Consequently, this method of collection must include a high degree of deniability regarding the information collected and the methods used to collect it.

Upon successful collection, raw data enter the processing stage, which is sometimes referred to as "processing and exploitation." Depending on the type of information collected, analysts may need to translate or decrypt the raw information into a form that helps synthesize analysis. Next, intelligence professionals turn the gathered raw data into actionable intelligence. During the analysis and production stage, analysts are tasked with evaluating the data, in an effort to assess developing trends and forecast future events. This process is time consuming, consisting of multiple possibilities being assessed per event, so as to consider all possible outcomes. Analytical assessments are then evaluated with statements of confidence and likelihood—terminology used by intelligence professionals to communicate the likelihood and credibility of sources and information—to aid in the dissemination of the product to the customer. One of the most important parts of this stage is the absence of bias or influence, since, as explained earlier, the task of intelligence analysts is to provide information, not to determine, or even advise toward, policy options. It follows that the customer, for example a senator, needs to be presented with unbiased information, as any bias, no matter how subtle, could potentially influence the outcome of the customer's overall decision.

Dissemination is arguably the most demanding and critical phase of the intelligence cycle. In the words of one expert, "this step can "make or break" the entire process" (Jensen et al., 2018). In this stage, the compiled and analyzed intelligence product is communicated to the agencies or professionals that the information was analyzed for. In an effort to hamper espionage efforts by adversaries, in 2008 Director of National Intelligence Mike McConnell reinforced the policy of "responsibility to provide" (Brewin, 2008). This means that intelligence products are communicated only to those that are tasked with receiving the information. Dissemination also poses the risk of adversaries intercepting and exploiting finished intelligence products to further their own aims, making security a major priority at this stage. Finished intelligence products will be briefed to policy- or decision-makers in either a written or oral briefing. The importance or usefulness of the information is ultimately decided by the customer.

Pandemic-Related Warnings in Recent Intelligence Products

The earliest known intelligence product that specifically describes a health pandemic similar to SARS-CoV-2 is contained in a 2004 estimative report from the National Intelligence Council (NIC). The NIC operates under the Office of the Director of National

Intelligence (ODNI), which is the coordinating body of the US IC (Office of the Director of National Intelligence, 2018b). Its primary mission is to provide American policy- and decision-makers with long-term strategic analysis of existing and emerging threats. The NIC report, entitled *Mapping the Global Future*, offers a descriptive projection of security threats the world could face by 2020. It states that it is "only a matter of time before a new pandemic appears, such as the 1918–1919 influenza virus that killed an estimated 20 million worldwide" (United States National Intelligence Council, 2004a). That assessment was sparked by security concerns raised by the 2002 coronavirus Severe Acute Respiratory Syndrome (SARS) outbreak in China. The NIC reiterated its assessment in 2008, when it issued its Global Trends 2025 report; it features an entire section discussing the possibility of a global pandemic. Notably, the section describes a now-familiar scenario, centering on "the emergence of a novel, highly transmissible, and virulent human respiratory illness for which there are no adequate countermeasures" (United States National Intelligence Council, 2004b). While the report sees such a pandemic as likely being caused by a pathogen like the Highly Pathogenic Asian Avian Influenza A (H5N1), it warns that "pathogens such as the SARS coronavirus or other influenza strains also have this potential" (United States National Intelligence Council, 2004b). The report also indicates that such an outbreak would likely originate in China, as it is a densely populated country were humans live in close quarters with livestock.

In 2012, amidst the outbreak of the Middle East Respiratory Syndrome (MERS), the NIC published *Global Trends 2035*. The report describes a global pandemic as a "black swan," and states bleakly that

> [a]n easily transmissible novel respiratory pathogen that kills or incapacitates more than one percent of its victims is among the most disruptive events possible. Such an outbreak could result in millions of people suffering and dying in every corner of the world in less than six months (United States National Intelligence Council, 2012).

Expressed concerns of the threat of a global pandemic are not contained solely in NIC reports. On the contrary, similar warnings were communicated for over a decade via the Worldwide Threat Assessment. Known officially as the Worldwide Threat Assessment of the US Intelligence Community, this annual intelligence product provides a summary of current and emerging threats to US national security. It is produced annually for use by the US Senate Select Committee on Intelligence, which in turn makes it available to the White House. In its "Human Security" section, the 2013 edition of the report states that

> humans will continue to be vulnerable to pandemics, most of which will probably originate in animals. An easily transmissible, novel respiratory pathogen that kills, or incapacitates more than one percent of its victims is among the most disruptive events possible. Such an outbreak would result in a global pandemic that causes suffering and death in every corner of the world, probably in fewer than six months (Office of the Director of National Intelligence, 2013).

This statement appears to forecast with remarkable accuracy the place of origin and mode of global transmission of SARS-CoV-2. Further on, the report employs stark language to caution policy-makers, stating that "[t]his is not a hypothetical threat. History is replete with examples of pathogens sweeping populations that lack immunity, causing political and economic upheaval, and influencing the outcomes of wars" (Office of the Director of National Intelligence, 2013). Similar threats were discussed in the 2015 edition of the Worldwide Threat Assessment, which states that "infectious diseases are among the foremost health security threats. A more crowded and interconnected world is increasing the opportunities for human and animal diseases to emerge and spread globally" (Office of the Director of National Intelligence, 2015). It is notable that the mounting concerns of the IC about a global pandemic were largely driven by the unparalleled growth of a globalized transportation infrastructure.

The annual Worldwide Threat Assessment reports have not only elaborated on the potential of a highly damaging health pandemic, but have also cautioned that the international community is not adequately prepared for such an event. This was noted in the 2016 assessment, which suggests that "the international community remains ill prepared to collectively coordinate and respond to disease threats" (Office of the Director of National Intelligence, 2016). Similar concerns were projected again in 2018, where we read about the possibility that a global health pandemic could lead to "a strain on governmental and international resources, and increase calls on the United States for support" (Office of the Director of National Intelligence, 2018a). The most recent Worldwide Threat Assessment, produced in 2019, specifically notes that current global health security regimes may not be sufficiently effective in the event of a global pandemic. The assessment includes the statement: "[a]lthough the international community has made tenuous improvements to global health security, these gains may be inadequate" (Office of the Director of National Intelligence, 2019).

In addition to the above strategic-intelligence products, which were made available to presidential administrations dating back to 2004, other elements of the US government have discussed repeatedly in recent years the potentially catastrophic effects of a global pandemic. In 2017, a Department of Defense pandemic and influenza response plan, which was drafted following the MERS coronavirus, stated that "the most likely significant pathogen threat is a novel respiratory disease, particularly a novel influenza disease" (United States Northern Command, 2017a). More recently, press reports have suggested that both the CIA and the Defense Intelligence Agency briefed senior officials in the Trump administration about the SARS-CoV-2 (Arciga, 2020). These briefings are believed to have taken place in early February, before the virus made its way into the US in a major way—though the question of whether the White House was briefed before COVID-19 arrived on American soil remains unanswered for the time being, given that the precise timing that the virus' entry into the US is itself under debate (Arciga, 2020).

The intelligence products discussed above demonstrate a clearly discernible evolution in the language used by their authors to alert their customers. One can observe the terminology change from estimative and speculative in feel at first, to gradually formulating direct warnings about the catastrophic consequences of a pandemic. Overall, it is clear that these concerns grew substantially in the 15 years following 2004 and the publication of *Mapping the Global Future*. Furthermore, the evolution of the language in these reports provides strong evidence of a growing trajectory of apprehension among disease-intelligence experts. By 2018, these experts were openly sounding the alarm about the threat of a global pandemic caused by a respiratory virus.

Intelligence products disseminated in the early stages of that period tend to discuss the broader context of pandemic threats, such as their effects on globalization. For instance, in a section titled "The Contradiction of Globalization," the National Intelligence Council's 2004 report, *Mapping the Global Future*, highlights the rapid expansion of globalization due to Chinese and Indian economic liberalization, the collapse of the USSR, and the technological revolution of the information era. It argues that the rapid advancements in globalization could simultaneously hinder, and even reverse, the process if certain events, such a pandemic, were to unfold. The report characteristically states that: "experts believe it is only a matter of time before a new pandemic appears, such as the 1918–1919 influenza virus that killed an estimated 20 million worldwide" (United States National Intelligence Council, 2004b). The analysts plainly articulate their greatest concerns regarding a pandemic, namely the human death toll and the adverse impact on the world economy. They also note that globalization would be threatened "if the death toll rose into the millions in several major countries and the spread of the disease put a halt to global travel and trade during an extended period" (United States National Intelligence Council, 2004b).

The context discussed in these earlier reports lays the foundation that successive Worldwide Threat Assessment releases stand on from 2008 onward. In sections titled "PLA Modernization," and "Infectious Disease and US Security," the 2008 report points to concerns about China's "high incidence of chronic and infectious disease" (McConnell, 2008), and even raises alarms about the United States' insufficient response to prior disease outbreaks, such as the avian H5N1 ("swine flu") virus. The 2009 edition of the Worldwide Threat Assessment expands upon the threat of a pandemic, by including a section titled "Global Health." As late as 2014, a full decade following the initial warnings issued by the NIC, Director of National Intelligence James R. Clapper continued to insist that, if a novel respiratory pathogen that had the ability to kill or incapacitate more than 1 percent of its victims were to become easily transmissible, "the outcome would be among the most disruptive events possible" (Clapper, 2015).

In another notable instance, the ODNI's 2017 Worldwide Threat Assessment explicitly notes that "a novel or remerging microbe that is easily transmissible between humans remains a major threat because such an organism has the potential to spread rapidly and kill millions." The 2018 edition of the report includes a similar statement about the next health pandemic, which can be described as a direct warning, rather than a precautionary comment. The warning explicitly mentions a strain of coronaviruses as potentially being responsible for causing the next health pandemic (Office of the Director of National Intelligence, 2018a). Shortly after that report was issued, the NSC's director of medical and biodefense preparedness warned that the threat of a pandemic flu was the world's foremost health security concern, something that the US was not prepared for (Sun, 2018).

Also in 2017, the Department of Defense's *US Northern Command Branch Plan 3560: Pandemic Influence and Infectious Disease Response* was published, based on an earlier plan drafted in 2006. The document is in essence a policy draft that details the US military's response to the causes of disease in humans. It describes in stark language how "a catastrophic biological incident could threaten the Nation's human, animal, plant, environmental, and economic health, as well as America's national security" (United States Northern Command, 2017b). The report goes into acute detail, discussing the strategic capabilities of the US military, a classification system for sorting the types of diseases and their methods of transmission, as well as the agencies responsible for the various stages of plans, establishing a chain of command in the event of an outbreak of "unique or novel pathogens" (United States Northern Command, 2017b).

In January of 2019, the ODNI's Worldwide Threat Assessment again included a warning about the next global health pandemic, this time explicitly stating that the US remained extremely vulnerable to the next pandemic. In September of 2019, the President's Council of Economic Advisors warned that the next pandemic would cause great economic damage and loss of life (Council of Economic Advisors, 2019). The following month, the DHHS concluded that the US biodefense infrastructure was underfunded, underprepared, undercoordinated, and generally incapable of combatting a flu-like pandemic as determined by a precautionary exercise (Sanger, 2019). Finally, between late November and early December of 2019, the Department of Defense's National Center for Medical Intelligence warned of a rapidly spreading and novel virus in Wuhan, China (Margolin and Meek, 2020).

Dismissal and Inaction by the Trump White House

In 2018, on the day after the NSC's director of medical and biodefense preparedness warned about the threat of a pandemic flu and the US' lack of preparedness, he was removed from his position and was never replaced. In the same breath, the NSC disbanded its Global Health Security Team overnight. Only days following that development, two members of the House Committee on Foreign Affairs wrote a letter to the President's National Security Advisor, expressing concern that the recent actions of the NSC "downgraded the importance of health security in the US" (Connolly and

Bera, 2018). These moves signaled major departures from the pandemic-related preparedness planning of prior administrations, including that of George W. Bush Jr., which was the first to develop a nationwide global health pandemic response plan (The White House, 2007). That plan was put in motion shortly after the NIC released its *Mapping the Global Future* report mentioned earlier, which explicitly discussed the threat of a global health pandemic. In November of 2005, President Bush delivered a speech on his plan, entitled "National Strategy for Pandemic Influenza Preparedness and Response" (The White House, 2007), in which he highlighted three key elements of that plan, which his administration saw as the most critical. The first element was the importance of bio-surveillance, which would ensure the early detection of viruses occurring anywhere in the world. The second element was the need to develop a national stockpile of critical virus-fighting vaccines and antiviral drugs, and to increase the nation's capability of developing new vaccines at faster rates. The third key element centered on the importance of pandemic preparedness at all levels of government, to include federal, state, and local (The White House, 2007).

To achieve these goals, in May of 2006 the Bush administration officially released its National Strategy for Pandemic Influenza Implementation Plan—a national security plan to combat the threat of a global health pandemic. In addition to that step, the Bush administration continued to fund the World Health Organization (WHO) Global Outbreak Alert and Response Network. It also invested in state and local government outbreak preparedness plans and developed a plan for dispersing critical medical resources in the event that they became scarce (The White House, 2007). In its reports, the Bush White House noted there were areas in pandemic preparedness that would continue to be in need in the coming years. Some of these areas included: strengthening US capabilities in clinical bio-surveillance, so as to better-detect outbreaks within the United States; strengthening medical capacity in order to properly care for and treat patients in the event of a pandemic; and continuing to work with international agencies like the WHO so as to properly prepare on a global scale for a health pandemic (The White House, 2007). These efforts by the Bush administration closely mirrored the critical developments proposed in relevant intelligence reports made available to the White House.

The major elements of the pandemic preparedness planning by the administration of President Barack Obama are highlighted in a cumulative report entitled Playbook for Early Response to High-Consequence Emerging Infectious Disease Threats and Biological Incidents (United States National Security Council, 2015). This report, better known as "The Pandemic Playbook," was produced by the National Security Council toward the end of the Obama administration, with the expressed purpose of passing on strategic pandemic preparedness knowledge to the incoming Trump administration (Knight, 2020). This publicly available document describes at length various pandemic preparedness procedures and includes a guide on how to assess public health threats, descriptions of how various pathogens originate and spread, and numerous charts to guide in risk assessments. It also highlights and describes the threat of a "novel coronavirus" similar to the current COVID-19 pandemic (Knight, 2020). The most pronounced distinction between the Bush and Obama administration's plans on pandemic preparedness is that the Obama administration's "Pandemic Playbook" focuses heavily on tracking a pathogen with pandemic potential before it poses an imminent threat to the United States—something that represents a clear enhancement of the previously available planning model. This appears to have been implemented in direct response to preparedness and containment shortcomings that the IC's Worldwide Threat Assessment indicated.

In 2017, just days after the inauguration of Donald Trump as the 45th president of the United States, officials from the Trump and Obama administrations participated in a pandemic preparedness exercise. The goal of the exercise was for the departing officials to inform their incoming counterparts of existing policies in the "Pandemic Playbook," which were designed to respond to a national health crisis. Most Trump administration officials who attended that exercise were no longer in office by the time of the outbreak of SARS-CoV-2 (Sun, 2018). Later that year, the Trump administration decided not to adopt the "Pandemic Playbook" created by Obama administration officials. Instead, it created its own pandemic preparedness plan, which is called the Pandemic Influenza Plan and is a product of the DHHS.

Shortly after developing its Pandemic Influenza Plan, the White House proposed a total of $277 million in budget cuts affecting the government's pandemic preparedness program. The plan included cutting $136 million from the Office of Public Health Preparedness and Response, $65 million from the National Center for Emerging and Zoonotic Infectious Diseases, and $76 million from the Centers of Disease Control and Prevention's (CDC) Center for Global Health (Baumgaertner, 2017). These cuts were rejected by Congress in May of 2017, but on February of next year the Trump administration did manage to withdraw $1.25 billion in funding from the CDC's Public Health Fund (Sun, 2018). On April 10, 2018, President' Trump's newly hired National Security Advisor, John Bolton, dismissed the White House's Homeland Security Advisor, days after he had called for "a comprehensive biodefense strategy against biological attacks and pandemics" (Toosi et al., 2020). Budget cuts continued in the coming year, with the White House proposing once again a budget cut of $252 billion for global health. In May 2018, these efforts prompted a letter to the president from Senator Sherrod Brown, who expressed concern that cutting federal and global health and pandemic preparedness budgets could "cost American lives" (Goodman and Schulkin, 2020). In September of that year, on orders from the president, the DHHS diverted $266 million from the CDC to the Unaccompanied Alien Children program, which provides housing for detained immigrant children (Goodman and Schulkin, 2020). That same month, the president announced the launch of a new "National Biodefense Strategy" and the creation of a Biodefense Coordination to "ensure a comprehensive and coordinate approach to biological incidents" (The White House, 2018). That strategy closely models the response plan implemented by the 2004 Bush administration, by highlighting the need for a well-stocked national stockpile of critical medical equipment, accelerating vaccine production capabilities, and increasing pathogen detection capabilities, specifically for influenza viruses (The White House, 2018). However, as we have seen, this plan failed to materialize in the critical early stages of the SARS-CoV-2 pandemic.

Discussion: SARS-CoV-2 and Intelligence Communication

The actions of the Trump administration in the years leading to the novel coronavirus outbreak reveal a systematic demotion of pandemic preparedness at the level of national strategy. They also provide a telling context for the administration's inaction in the early stages of the outbreak. It is therefore difficult—indeed impossible—to propose a forensic evaluation of America's response to COVID-19 without placing a significant portion of the responsibility on the door of the White House. The question, however, remains, and is at the heart of the issue: why were the warnings of the IC not heeded by the president and his administration? We believe that this query can be addressed on multiple levels, including political, economic, and even cultural. At least one of them, however involves the role of the IC in protecting American national security, specifically through the dissemination of intelligence, which, as explained earlier, is arguably the most critical step of the intelligence cycle. Addressing this issue is vital for the future of American national security, because it points to the desperate need for efficient communication between the IC and the highest levels of government, especially on matters of critical importance to the safety of the nation.

It has become apparent to intelligence agencies that the communications revolution in our century has multiplied the channels of readily available information that are available to consumers of intelligence (Liaropoulos, 2006). As a result, US intelligence finds itself operating today in "an extraordinarily competitive environment," in which it is "competing for business, and consumers" (Degaut, 2016). The latter are now increasingly questioning the value of intelligence products given to them, and constantly compare these products to a host of open-source channels of information, such as 24-h television news, as well as Internet sites. This tendency has arguably seen its culmination with President Trump. According to insiders like Susan Gordon, until recently Principal Deputy Director of National Intelligence, the president is known to consistently confront his intelligence briefers with comments such as: "I don't think that's true" or "I'm not sure I believe that," even when presented with conclusive evidence on a topic of concern (Gordon, 2019). This potentially points to a breakdown in communication between the IC and the president, during meetings that are often combative and cut short due to the president's other obligations.

This growing problem is compounded by what former senior CIA Directorate of Intelligence officer Martin Petersen describes as "the most precious commodity in Washington"—not information, of which there is an abundance, "but time" (Petersen, 2011). Decision-makers understand the importance of being informed. However, their scarcity of time forces them to prioritize sources of information that offer easily digestible analyses with immediacy and certainty. This poses major challenges for authors of finished intelligence products, who tend to prioritize quality over speed. Unlike the raw information collected by intelligence agencies, finished intelligence products are meticulously analyzed so as to lessen the degree of uncertainty of a particular issue. Consequently, they rarely—if ever—present the reader with absolute answers to questions, which makes them appear inconclusive. It is therefore imperative that the IC places emphasis on the speed of communication between it and key consumers as a matter of policy. A major way of facilitating increased immediacy is by focusing less on "the incremental addition of new intelligence from human sources or technical sensors" (Hulnick, 2006) and more on already available data to answer questions. According to former CIA intelligence analyst Hulnick, such a methodology is realistic, given that existing data "is already so large that a competent analyst could write about most events without any more than open sources to spur the process" (Hulnick, 2006).

The time-constraint factor in intelligence communication is especially prevalent in interactions between the IC and the president. Since 1946, American presidents have been the main recipients of what has been described as "the finest intelligence publication in the world" (Wilder, 2011), namely the President's Daily Brief (PDB). The PDB provides the president, and a small number of senior officials selected by the president, with snippets of current intelligence on pressing global developments. It is produced by the ODNI in coordination with the President's Analytic Support Staff of the CIA Directorate of Analysis, and contains descriptive and estimative reports based on information provided by practically every agency in the IC. Reports in the press have stated that President Trump received information about the novel coronavirus through the PDB. According to these reports, successive PDBs "raised the prospect of dire political and economic consequences" with a frequency that "reflected a level of attention comparable to periods when analysts have been tracking active terrorism threats, overseas conflicts or other rapidly developing security issues" (Miller, G., 2020). However, the degree to which the PDB can be expected to deliver warning intelligence to the president is questionable. According to CIA analysts, the PDB is typically viewed by intelligence managers and decision-makers alike as "educational in nature," and "not [...] the kind of intelligence product used for warning" (Hulnick, 2006). Moreover, decision-makers often find it difficult to focus on the details contained in PDBs, due to their highly specific and technical nature. The latter contrasts with the abstract and strategic mode of thinking that presidents and other senior officials are accustomed to engage in. Consequently, it is often the case that the consumer of the PDB leaves the meeting without having retained the information that the briefer, as well as the authoring analysts, view as paramount (Wolfberg, 2014).

The unpredictability and arbitrariness of PDB encounters only increases when the consumer is someone like President Trump, who has admittedly limited experience in statecraft or intelligence matters. Trump's background in these fields lacks in comparison to most prior presidents, including, for instance, George Bush Sr., a former ambassador, who also served as director of the CIA before entering the Oval Office. Even in the best of times, PDB meetings are awkward and involve "both briefer and policymaker [sitting] down in the same room, physically near each other, while the policymaker reads the written material" (Wolfberg, 2014). The consumer peruses the material "under the gaze of the briefer," who is often reduced to "carefully [watching] the policymakers' gestures, body language, and facial expressions," following "the policymaker's eyes, attempting to detect which sections the policymaker [is] spending the most amount of time on reading" and even paying "attention to the pattern the policymaker's finger [makes] as he or she [views] each page of the briefing book" (Wolfberg, 2014). The awkwardness of this mostly silent exchange is compounded by the pressing schedule the consumer is under, which inevitably leads to "difficulty in absorbing all the material in the briefing book" during the relatively short PDB meeting. Inevitably, therefore, policymakers filter the information, "paying attention to some things, ignoring other things" (Wolfberg, 2014).

It should also be noted that, even though the PDB is delivered to the consumer in a written format, many presidents expect to be guided through the document orally by the briefer. President Trump has been repeatedly criticized in the press for allegedly having a "style of learning" that does not involve reading. The president is alleged to have eventually made it clear to his briefer that "he was not interested in reviewing a personal copy of the written intelligence report known as the PDB." Instead, he has relied on exclusively "oral sessions," according to administration officials (Leonnig, 2018). This has been seen as a radical—even alarming—

departure from established practice, and must have been looked down upon by the IC, where the prevailing notion has always been that "policymakers who do not devote time on a regular basis to read intelligence reports [...] are clearly not doing their jobs" (Degaut, 2016). It is equally true, however, that "[t]he history of the PDB is one of flexibility and remarkable adaptation of support to fit each president's needs and information acquisition styles" (Wilder, 2011). This statement, made by an IC insider, implies that it is the IC's briefing conventions that must adapt to the consumer's style of retaining and digesting the information, rather than the other way around. It also points to further communication breakdown between President Trump and his IC briefers—an unfortunate state of affairs that may be at least partially responsible for the administration's slow response to the novel coronavirus pandemic. We can thus infer that, as has been reported in the press, PDBs in November and December of 2019 made repeated mentions of COVID-19. By that time, however, the president was viewing the product as, in the words of former CIA analyst Martin Petersen, "optional equipment" (Petersen, 2011).

How can this problem be corrected? We believe that the PDB continues to be an efficient method for communicating current intelligence to the highest levels of government. However, as the COVID-19 experience shows, this mode of intelligence communication cannot serve as an effective warning mechanism. The same can be stated for the myriad of in-depth intelligence reports produced annually by the analytic components of the IC, such as Global Trends and the Worldwide Threat Assessment. As Hulnick has remarked, these intelligence products are "meant more for policy officials at working levels rather than senior decision makers, who rarely have the time to read them" (Hulnick, 2006). Like the PDB, these annual reports cannot be seen as replacing what the IC refers to as "deep dives," namely in-depth presentations on pressing matters of concern that bring together decision-makers with the IC's domain experts, rather than just trained briefers (Wolfberg, 2014). Such deep dives—30-min to an hour-long interactive sessions on specific topics of concern—must become more prevalent as a form of strategic communication between the IC and key customers. Moreover, we believe that the IC must give serious thought to the possibility of producing a separate version of the PDB that will focus strictly on warning intelligence— that is, critical information on topics that are not on the radar of decision-makers. This version of the PDB—let us call it the President's Critical Brief, or PCB—does not need to be produced daily, though it should be disseminated at least weekly. Additionally, it should concentrate heavily on catastrophic and existential threats to national security, including threats by new and unfamiliar actors, large-scale biosecurity concerns, weapons of mass destruction, climate change indicators, and other similar topics.

Lastly, we propose a thorough reconsideration of the principle of preventing IC analysts from proposing policy options to decision-makers. As explained earlier, the line that divides the relaying of information from proposing policy options is engrained in the very operational modality of the US IC—though interestingly it is not a feature of intelligence work in other Western countries. However, the case of the novel coronavirus may point to the need to reconsider this division when it comes to topics that pose existential or otherwise catastrophic challenges to national security. As NSC analyst Dennis Wilder has astutely observed

> increasingly today, policymakers and legislators find that the intelligence analysts' adherence to this article of faith robs the policymaker of the ideas and suggestions for policy that a highly informed analyst can provide (Wilder, 2011).

The reasoning that informs this "article of faith," as Wilder calls it, is a sound one—namely the need to preserve the intelligence analyst's political objectivity and professional integrity, by keeping them at arm's length from the policy domain. However, as Wilder notes, preventing an analytical expert from advising on policy—especially on threats of an existential nature—denies the policymaker "some of the most useful byproducts of analytic depth and sophistication" that the IC is known for Wilder (2011).

Conclusion: Toward an Effective Model of Intelligence Communication

The Trump administration is being untruthful when it portrays the novel coronavirus pandemic as a strategic surprise. Its assertions that COVID-19 "came out of nowhere" fly in the face of over 15 years of pandemic preparedness warnings by the IC. Moreover, such claims insult the intelligence professionals whose work has consistently informed the pandemic preparedness strategies of three presidential administrations, including President Trump's. Consequently, we believe that it is impossible to forensically evaluate the slow US response to the pandemic without placing much of the responsibility for it on the White House. It is equally impossible, however, to assess the inaction of the Trump administration without examining the deeper breakdown in strategic communication between key decision-makers and the IC. Indeed, the breakdown in communication between these two actors points to the urgent need to re-evaluate the standard methods of intelligence dissemination to the highest levels of government.

It is clear that, in the decade leading to 2020, the IC drew on over 70 years of experience in disease intelligence to warn policy- and decision-makers about the impending threat of a respiratory virus. These warnings became increasingly stark between 2014 and 2018, by which time IC experts were openly and directly sounding the alarm about what they correctly saw as an imminent threat. That the Trump administration downplayed pandemic preparedness as a matter of national policy is unquestionable. It is equally unquestionable, however, that the means of strategic communication employed by the IC to alert the White House to the threat were unproductive. These alerts were communicated largely through the PDB, an archaic and ineffectual method of communication, which is not typically seen as an instrument of warning. The awkwardness, unpredictability, and randomness of PDB exchanges do not facilitate the kind of laser-focused, unequivocal exchange of information that is needed when potentially catastrophic threats are upon the nation. Instead, the IC must implement communication methods that favor more direct, immediate and conclusive intelligence dissemination, and should seriously consider the creation of a new line of products that address existential and potentially catastrophic challenges to national security. Lastly, we believe it is high time to reconsider the division between intelligence reporting and policy advising. We agree with the view that intelligence analysts should stay clear of providing policy advice during routine reporting to customers. However, we do not see the value of preventing highly knowledgeable and capable intelligence professionals from offering policy advice to decision-makers when it comes to threats that are considered catastrophic or potentially existential for the US and its people.

CHAPTER 2

Are Science and Politics at Odds with One Another?

Overview: Politicians Should Not Dismiss Science

Mauktik Kulkarni

Mauktik Kulkarni is an author, filmmaker, and neuroscientist.

The COVID-19 pandemic has surpassed 9/11 as the defining moment of our generation. Due to the singular nature of this scare, global heads of state are in need of sound advice from scientists. In these surreal times, it is worth examining the relationship of science with politics, and the importance of a scientific temper. Science and politics are generally at odds. Science proposes hypotheses, develops replicable tools to test them out, and generates verifiable facts. Politicians weave facts into narratives that a majority is willing to buy into. While American scientists like Anthony Fauci have become overnight heroes, they are unelected appointees. Conversely, politicians are answerable to their electorates.

There is no dearth of politics in science, and it is not infallible as an intellectual discipline, but what does science tell us about politics? We belong to the only species that has designed democratic systems and goes beyond physical superiority while choosing leaders. Franklin D. Roosevelt, Mahatma Gandhi, or Nelson Mandela led with their soaring rhetoric, strategic planning, empathy, and sacrifice. These traits could be attributed to brain regions like the pre-frontal cortex, which is not only the seat of complex emotional analysis, it lets us understand causal chains and plan for the future. It enables us to suppress primal instincts like fight-or-flight responses, look beyond our self-interest, and appeal to collective humanity, uniquely empowering us to fight off common threats. Good leaders can relieve anxiety, synthesize emerging data, implement public health strategies, and summon

"Science and Politics Should Not Be at Odds," by Mauktik Kulkarni, LiveMint, April 18, 2020. Reprinted by permission.

our higher angels, so to speak. Populists, in contrast, rarely inspire the confidence needed in the face of an invisible but real threat like a virus.

Consider the response of various countries. By prioritizing national pride over public safety, Chinese leaders downplayed covid-19's severity, and resorted to what looked like obfuscation (Beijing has just revised Wuhan's death toll upwards). In the US, the stance of President Donald Trump has been bewildering, to say the least. He has lurched from crisis to crisis, vacillating on several issues, and this pandemic caught his administration first in denial of a health crisis and then unprepared to tackle it. He negated learnings from the 2014 Ebola outbreak and had disbanded the American pandemic response team. He ignored covid red flags raised by US intelligence agencies in January. Despite evidence from South Korea on the efficacy of mass testing, it was too late by the time the US ramped its efforts up. All along, he seemed to have a tin ear for scientists.

India's fate hangs in the balance too. It remains unclear how well the country had fared against the pandemic. Enlarged dividends from the Reserve Bank of India (RBI) would have been helpful in a crisis like this, as also a transfer of some RBI reserves, but the government had already resorted to this device in 2019-20 to cover gaps in public finances. In the early phase of the outbreak, India should have tested 8,000 people a day, but tested only about 100 per day till mid-March. The country's test count has risen sharply since then, but still remains very low on a test-per-million-population basis. The restrictions put in place before the 21-day lockdown were not properly implemented either.

Another worry is that government authorities do not seem to command everyone's trust equally, an outcome of divisive politics in the country. This diminishes the state's capacity for mass mobilization against covid. Announcements by the health ministry of cases being traced to a religious congregation of the Tablighi Jamaat in Delhi did not help the cause of forging unity among all citizens.

The lockdown in itself was a promising step. It may have achieved some of it goals in slowing down covid's spread, but when the curve of infections will flatten cannot yet to projected with confidence. Regardless, the pandemic has dealt a huge blow to the government's desire to make India a $5 trillion economy by 2024-25.

The success of a country eventually comes down to the adoption of a scientific temper in public affairs. The 20th century has shown that societies at the forefront of scientific prowess and fearless inquiry tend to lead the world. After a glorious run after World War II, America's conservatives appear to be ceding its scientific leadership by doubting the motivations of experts. Trump's antics embody the abandonment of a scientific temper. His mismanagement has worsened the US covid crisis. Indian conservatives, on the other hand, seem intent on glorifying their past even before the country can demonstrate beyond dispute that it is home to a truly forward-thinking society. What we ought to expect are daily updates on the spread of the coronavirus, and technical details of our efforts to address the crisis, backed by health experts, rather than exhortations to clap and light candles. The apparent lack of public pressure on the government to answer specific queries on covid-19 reflects the state of scientific temper in India.

State-level leaders are filling the void. In sombre tones, they are providing facts and figures, announcing plans for the needy, or conveying the latest from scientists. It takes such straight talk to unify all constituents. People empowered with verifiable information are willing to make collective sacrifices. Some leaders will ride out the pandemic's aftermath, and some will not. Let us hope the politics of tomorrow restores science to its rightful place in society.

Deadly Lies Were the Norm in the 2020 Pandemic

Daniel Funke and Katie Sanders

Daniel Funke is a staff writer for PolitiFact and covers online misinformation. Katie Sanders is the managing editor of PolitiFact.

A Florida taxi driver and his wife had seen enough conspiracy theories online to believe the virus was overblown, maybe even a hoax. So no masks for them. Then they got sick. She died. A college lecturer had trouble refilling her lupus drug after the president promoted it as a treatment for the new disease. A hospital nurse broke down when an ICU patient insisted his illness was nothing worse than the flu, oblivious to the silence in beds next door.

Lies infected America in 2020. The very worst were not just damaging, but deadly.

President Donald Trump fueled confusion and conspiracies from the earliest days of the coronavirus pandemic. He embraced theories that COVID-19 accounted for only a small fraction of the thousands upon thousands of deaths. He undermined public health guidance for wearing masks and cast Dr. Anthony Fauci as an unreliable flip-flopper.

But the infodemic was not the work of a single person.

Anonymous bad actors offered up junk science. Online skeptics made bogus accusations that hospitals padded their coronavirus case numbers to generate bonus payments. Influential TV and radio opinion hosts told millions of viewers that physical distancing was a joke and that states had all of the personal protective equipment they needed (when they didn't).

"Lie of the Year: The Downplay and Denial of the Coronavirus," by Daniel Funke and Katie Sanders, KHN and PolitiFact Health Check, December 16, 2020. Reprinted by permission.

It was a symphony of counter-narrative, and Trump was the conductor, if not the composer. The message: The threat to your health was overhyped to hurt the political fortunes of the president.

Every year, PolitiFact editors review the year's most inaccurate statements to elevate one as the Lie of the Year. The "award" goes to a statement, or a collection of claims, that prove to be of substantive consequence in undermining reality.

It has become harder and harder to choose when cynical pundits and politicians don't pay much of a price for saying things that aren't true. For the past month, unproven claims of massive election fraud have tested democratic institutions and certainly qualify as historic and dangerously baldfaced. Fortunately, the constitutional foundations that undergird American democracy are holding.

Meanwhile, the coronavirus has killed more than 300,000 in the United States, a crisis exacerbated by the reckless spread of falsehoods.

PolitiFact's 2020 Lie of the Year: claims that deny, downplay or disinform about COVID-19.

"I Wanted to Always Play It Down"

On Feb. 7, Trump leveled with book author Bob Woodward about the dangers of the new virus that was spreading across the world, originating in central China. He told the legendary reporter that the virus was airborne, tricky and "more deadly than even your strenuous flus."

Trump told the public something else. On Feb. 26, the president appeared with his coronavirus task force in the crowded White House briefing room. A reporter asked if he was telling healthy Americans not to change their behavior.

"Wash your hands, stay clean. You don't have to necessarily grab every handrail unless you have to," he said, the room chuckling. "I mean, view this the same as the flu."

Three weeks later, March 19, he acknowledged to Woodward: "To be honest with you, I wanted to always play it down. I still like playing it down. Because I don't want to create a panic."

His acolytes in politics and the media were on the same page. Rush Limbaugh told his audience of about 15 million on Feb. 24 that the coronavirus was being weaponized against Trump when it was just "the common cold, folks." That's wrong—even in the early weeks, it was clear the virus had a higher fatality rate than the common cold, with worse potential side effects, too.

As the virus was spreading, so was the message to downplay it.

"There are lots of sources of misinformation, and there are lots of elected officials besides Trump that have not taken the virus seriously or promoted misinformation," said Brendan Nyhan, a government professor at Dartmouth College. "It's not solely a Trump story—and it's important to not take everyone else's role out of the narrative."

Hijacking the Numbers

In August, there was a growing movement on Twitter to question the disproportionately high US COVID-19 death toll.

The skeptics cited Centers for Disease Control and Prevention data to claim that only 6% of COVID-19 deaths could actually be attributed to the virus. On Aug. 24, BlazeTV host Steve Deace amplified it on Facebook.

"Here's the percentage of people who died OF or FROM Covid with no underlying comorbidity," he said to his 120,000 followers. "According to CDC, that is just 6% of the deaths WITH Covid so far."

That misrepresented the reality of coronavirus deaths. The CDC had always said people with underlying health problems—comorbidities—were most vulnerable if they caught COVID-19. The report was noting that 6% died even without being at obvious risk.

But for those skeptical of COVID-19, the narrative confirmed their beliefs. Facebook users copied and pasted language from influencers like Amiri King, who had 2.2 million Facebook followers before he was banned. The Gateway Pundit called it a "SHOCK REPORT."

"I saw a statistic come out the other day, talking about only 6% of the people actually died from COVID, which is very interesting—that they died from other reasons," Trump told Fox News host Laura Ingraham on Sept. 1.

Fauci, director of the National Institute of Allergy and Infectious Diseases, addressed the claim on "Good Morning America" the same day.

"The point that the CDC was trying to make was that a certain percentage of them had nothing else but just COVID," he said. "That does not mean that someone who has hypertension or diabetes who dies of COVID didn't die of COVID-19—they did."

Trump retweeted the message from an account that sported the slogans and symbols of QAnon, a conspiracy movement that claims Democrats and Hollywood elites are members of an underground pedophilia ring.

False information moved between social media, Trump and TV, creating its own feedback loop.

"It's an echo effect of sorts, where Donald Trump is certainly looking for information that resonates with his audiences and that supports his political objectives. And his audiences are looking to be amplified, so they're incentivized to get him their information," said Kate Starbird, an associate professor and misinformation expert at the University of Washington.

Weakening the Armor: Misleading on Masks

At the start of the pandemic, the CDC told healthy people not to wear masks, saying they were needed for health care providers on the front lines. But on April 3 the agency changed its guidelines, saying every American should wear non-medical cloth masks in public.

Trump announced the CDC's guidance, then gutted it.

"So it's voluntary. You don't have to do it. They suggested for a period of time, but this is voluntary," Trump said at a press briefing. "I don't think I'm going to be doing it."

Rather than an advance in best practices on coronavirus prevention, face masks turned into a dividing line between Trump's political calculations and his decision-making as president. Americans didn't see Trump wearing a mask until a July visit to Walter Reed National Military Medical Center.

Meanwhile, disinformers flooded the internet with wild claims: Masks reduced oxygen. Masks trapped fungus. Masks trapped coronavirus. Masks just didn't work.

In September, the CDC reported a correlation between people who went to bars and restaurants, where masks can't consistently be worn, and positive COVID-19 test results. Bloggers and skeptical news outlets countered with a misleading report about masks.

On Oct. 13, the story landed on Fox News' flagship show, "Tucker Carlson Tonight." During the show, Carlson claimed "almost everyone—85%—who got the coronavirus in July was wearing a mask."

"So clearly [wearing a mask] doesn't work the way they tell us it works," Carlson said.

That's wrong, and it misrepresented a small sample of people who tested positive. Public health officials and infectious disease experts have been consistent since April in saying that face masks are among the best ways to prevent the spread of COVID-19.

But two days later, Trump repeated the 85% stat during a rally and at a town hall with NBC's Savannah Guthrie.

"I tell people, wear masks," he said at the town hall. "But just the other day, they came out with a statement that 85% of the people that wear masks catch it."

The Assault on Hospitals

On March 24, registered nurse Melissa Steiner worked her first shift in the new COVID-19 ICU of her southeastern Michigan hospital. After her 13-hour workday caring for two critically ill patients on ventilators, she posted a tearful video.

"Honestly, guys, it felt like I was working in a war zone," Steiner said. "[I was] completely isolated from my team members, limited resources, limited supplies, limited responses from physicians because they're just as overwhelmed."

"I'm already breaking, so for f—'s sake, people, please take this seriously. This is so bad."

Steiner's post was one of many emotional pleas offered by overwhelmed hospital workers last spring urging people to take the threat seriously. The denialists mounted a counteroffensive.

On March 28, Todd Starnes, a conservative radio host and commentator, tweeted a video from outside Brooklyn Hospital Center. There were few people or cars in sight.

"This is the 'war zone' outside the hospital in my Brooklyn neighborhood," Starnes said sarcastically. The video racked up more than 1.5 million views.

Starnes' video was one of the first examples of #FilmYourHospital, a conspiratorial social media trend that pushed back on the idea that hospitals had been strained by a rapid influx of coronavirus patients.

Several internet personalities asked people to go out and shoot their own videos. The result: a series of user-generated clips taken outside hospitals, where the response to the pandemic was not easily seen. Over the course of a week, #FilmYourHospital videos were uploaded to YouTube and posted tens of thousands of times on Twitter and Facebook.

Nearly two weeks and more than 10,000 deaths later, Fox News featured a guest who opened a new misinformation assault on hospitals.

Dr. Scott Jensen, a Minnesota physician and Republican state senator, told Ingraham that, because hospitals were receiving more money for COVID-19 patients on Medicare—a result of a coronavirus stimulus bill—they were overcounting

COVID-19 cases. He had no proof of fraud, but the cynical story took off.

Trump used the false report on the campaign trail to continue to minimize the death toll.

"Our doctors get more money if somebody dies from COVID," Trump told supporters at a rally in Waterford, Michigan, on Oct. 30. "You know that, right? I mean, our doctors are very smart people. So what they do is they say, 'I'm sorry, but, you know, everybody dies of COVID.'"

The Real Fake News: The Plandemic

The most viral disinformation of the pandemic was styled to look as if it had the blessing of people Americans trust: scientists and doctors.

In a 26-minute video called "Plandemic: The Hidden Agenda Behind COVID-19," a former scientist at the National Cancer Institute claimed the virus was manipulated in a lab, hydroxychloroquine is effective against coronaviruses, and face masks make people sick.

Judy Mikovits' conspiracies received more than 8 million views, partly credited to the online outrage machine—anti-vaccine activists, anti-lockdown groups and QAnon supporters—that push disinformation into the mainstream. The video was circulated in a coordinated effort to promote Mikovits' book release.

Around the same time, a similar effort propelled another video of fact-averse doctors to millions of people in only a few hours.

On July 27, Breitbart published a clip of a press conference hosted by a group called America's Frontline Doctors in front of the US Supreme Court. Looking authoritative in white lab coats, these doctors discouraged mask-wearing and falsely said there was already a cure in hydroxychloroquine, a drug used to treat rheumatoid arthritis and lupus.

Trump, who had been talking up the drug since March and claimed to be taking it himself as a preventive measure in May, retweeted clips of the event before Twitter removed them as misinformation about COVID-19. He defended the "very respected doctors" in a July 28 press conference.

When Olga Lucia Torres, a lecturer at Columbia University, heard Trump touting the drug in March, she knew it didn't bode well for her own prescription. Sure enough, the misinformation led to a run on hydroxychloroquine, creating a shortage for Americans like her who needed the drug for chronic conditions.

A lupus patient, she went to her local pharmacy to request a 90-day supply of the medication. But she was told they were granting only partial refills. It took her three weeks to get her medication through the mail.

"What about all the people who were silenced and just lost access to their staple medication because people ran to their doctors and begged to take it?" Torres said.

No Sickbed Conversion

On Sept. 26, Trump hosted a Rose Garden ceremony to announce his nominee to replace the late Ruth Bader Ginsburg on the US Supreme Court. More than 150 people attended the event introducing Amy Coney Barrett. Few wore masks, and the chairs weren't spaced out.

In the weeks afterward, more than two dozen people close to Trump and the White House became infected with COVID-19. Early on Oct. 2, Trump announced his positive test.

Those hoping the experience and Trump's successful treatment at Walter Reed might inform his view of the coronavirus were disappointed. Trump snapped back into minimizing the threat during his first moments back at the White House. He yanked off his mask and recorded a video.

"Don't let it dominate you. Don't be afraid of it," he said, describing experimental and mostly out-of-reach therapies he received. "You're going to beat it."

In Trump's telling, his hospitalization was not the product of poor judgment about large gatherings like the Rose Garden event, but the consequence of leading with bravery. Plus, now, he claimed, he had immunity to the virus.

On the morning after he returned from Walter Reed, Trump tweeted a seasonal flu death count of 100,000 lives and added that COVID-19 was "far less lethal" for most populations. More false claims at odds with data—the US average for flu deaths over the past decade is 36,000, and experts said COVID-19 is more deadly for each age group over 30.

When Trump left the hospital, the US death toll from COVID-19 was more than 200,000. Today it is more than 300,000. Meanwhile, this month the president has gone ahead with a series of indoor holiday parties.

The Vaccine War

The vaccine disinformation campaign started in the spring but is still underway.

In April, blogs and social media users falsely claimed Democrats and powerful figures like Bill Gates wanted to use microchips to track which Americans had been vaccinated for the coronavirus. Now, false claims are taking aim at vaccines developed by Pfizer and BioNTech and other companies.

- A blogger claimed Pfizer's head of research said the coronavirus vaccine could cause female infertility. That's false.
- An alternative health website wrote that the vaccine could cause an array of life-threatening side effects, and that the FDA knew about it. The list included all possible—not confirmed—side effects.
- Social media users speculated that the federal government would force Americans to receive the vaccine. Neither Trump nor President-elect Joe Biden has advocated for that, and the federal government doesn't have the power to mandate vaccines, anyway.

As is often the case with disinformation, the strategy is to deliver it with a charade of certainty.

"People are anxious and scared right now," said Dr. Seema Yasmin, director of research and education programs at the Stanford Health Communication Initiative. "They're looking for a whole picture."

Most polls have shown far from universal acceptance of vaccines, with only 50% to 70% of respondents willing to take the vaccine. Black and Hispanic Americans are even less likely to take it so far.

Meanwhile, the future course of the coronavirus in the US depends on whether Americans take public health guidance to heart. The Institute for Health Metrics and Evaluation projected that, without mask mandates or a rapid vaccine rollout, the death toll could rise to more than 500,000 by April 2021.

"How can we come to terms with all that when people are living in separate informational realities?" Starbird said.

What Happens When We Prioritize Politics and Economics Over Science

Meridith McGraw and Nancy Cook

Meridith McGraw and Nancy Cook are both reporters at the White House and report for Politico.

T he coronavirus battle brewing inside the Trump administration is putting two urgent imperatives in conflict—showing credibility in tackling a global health crisis while calming unsettled investors and voters in an election year.

On Monday, one top White House official publicly disputed concerns about a market downturn while President Donald Trump commented directly on it. On Tuesday, health officials broadcast their expertise about the virus while Trump sought to quash such chatter. And on Wednesday, top aides debated publicly whether the administration would need a czar to coordinate a government response as the president announced a rare evening news conference and attacked the media.

Then Trump came striding out Wednesday night to the White House briefing room podium, attempting to clear things up. He tapped Vice President Mike Pence to helm the response and acquiesced to a bipartisan congressional demand for more emergency funding than the White House had previously requested. But his typical confidence and downplaying of the threat—he bragged that America was a top-ranked country for handling a viral outbreak and noted the seasonal flu was killing more people than the coronavirus—continued the administration's occasional discordant messaging on the subject.

"We're ready to adapt and do whatever we have to as the disease spreads, if it spreads," Trump said, making only his second appearance on the briefing room podium during his time in office.

"Trump's Coronavirus Conflict: Science vs. Politics," by Meridith McGraw and Nancy Cook, Politico, February 26, 2020. Reprinted by permission.

Widening fears about a potential health catastrophe are thrusting the Trump White House into a form of crisis management different from anything it has experienced in three years, pitting transparency against politics just as top officials hoped to be pivoting away from impeachment to the 2020 reelection fight.

Now, the White House is trying to project confidence about America's ability to contain the coronavirus—now present in 37 countries, but about which much remains unknown—while appearing prepared for an outbreak in the US. It's a tricky moment for any president to balance an image of both strength and caution, coming in a week when the administration's political messaging has seemed disorganized and often in conflict.

In an effort to appear in control of the response, the president told aides on Air Force One during his return trip from India that he wanted to hold Wednesday night's news conference. Secretary of Health and Human Services Alex Azar and other members of the coronavirus task force were expected to brief the president ahead of his appearance, which came hours after the stock market closed out another volatile day.

"President Trump realizes that people need to hear about the coronavirus from him," said Jason Miller, senior communications adviser on the 2016 Trump campaign. "The media environment he is returning to is different than when he left for India."

Miller said Trump needed to be surrounded by officials from the Centers for Disease Control and Prevention conveying basic concepts like who is at risk of contracting coronavirus and how Americans can avoid it.

"Even if the virus is not our fault, we will be the ones to solve the problem," Miller said. "That is the message the American people need to hear."

Trump's decision to appear as the face of the coronavirus response came after the president and officials the White House were "livid" with the statements made Tuesday by Nancy Messonnier, director of the CDC's National Center for Immunization and Respiratory Diseases. Her warning that a coronavirus outbreak in the United States was "not a question of if, but rather a question of when" raised alarm bells and contradicted the public messaging from the White House that the situation was serious, but under control.

On the same day, Director of the National Economic Council Larry Kudlow said on CNBC: "We have contained this, I won't say airtight but pretty close to airtight."

The White House tried to project a sense of confidence, and pointed to the president's early creation of a coronavirus task force, travel restrictions and a containment strategy.

But that was at odds with what federal officials have publicly warned could be a dire situation—messaging seen as credible by many lawmakers but slammed by the president's aides and allies.

"I don't understand how the CDC could make an announcement as important as yesterday without it being tightly coordinated with the [White House]," former President George W. Bush's press secretary, Ari Fleischer, said on Twitter. "There should have been an Oval Office meeting, a statement by POTUS about protecting people, and then a press avail by experts. Bizarre."

With criticism over the messaging mounting on Wednesday, the White House sent out talking points to allies praising the president's response as "aggressive and proactive."

"The Administration is taking aggressive and proactive measures, working closely with state and local partners to protect the public health," the document said. "President Trump has led the way in addressing the coronavirus and has allowed the US to stay ahead of the outbreak as it has developed."

Publicly, the president tried to show he had taken command and assured that Americans were safe.

"The risk to the American people remains very low," he said. "We have the greatest experts really in the world."

But behind the scenes, officials have prepared for scenarios in which the virus could spread out of control—especially in densely populated and poor areas abroad. It's not known exactly how many people are affected in Iran, but an unofficial report published by

Canadian researchers was circulated among some officials inside the White House that predicted as many as 18,000 cases—a number seen as within the realm of possibility.

The National Security Council held a table-top exercise last week in which officials went through potential scenarios and mapped out needs in the case of any spike in cases.

An administration official also said the White House was considering measures that included travel restrictions for South Korea and Italy. The CDC already raised its travel advisory for South Korea to the highest level, recommending that travelers avoid all nonessential travel, but Italy still remains at the level below.

Trump on Wednesday took credit for an early decision to ban certain travelers from China shortly after the virus outbreak began.

"A lot of people thought we shouldn't have done it that early," he said.

Senior administration officials have stressed in recent days that the president's decision early on to shut down flights between the US and China gave the administration much-needed time to ramp up vaccine development, explore potential treatments and examine possible disruptions to supply chains for US companies.

"Unfortunately what we are seeing is a political effort by the Left and some in the media to distract and disturb the American people with fearful rhetoric and palace intrigue," White House spokesman Judd Deere said in a statement. "The virus remains low-risk domestically because of the containment actions taken by this Administration since the first of the year."

"The global situation is serious and changing hourly, which is exactly why Secretary Azar continues to lead a whole-of-government response in partnership with state and local leaders that includes the best experts on infectious diseases," Deere said. "It's also exactly why the White House is requesting from Congress $2.5 billion in funding to accelerate vaccine development and further support preparedness and response efforts. The President is receiving regular updates, and is prepared to take additional action to protect the American people."

White House aides have long wanted the public message on the coronavirus to delve into the public health concerns rather than the potential economic damage. But behind the scenes, aides have been running models of the possible impact on both the US and global economies. The US stock market took major tumbles Monday and Tuesday after the coronavirus spread to both Italy and Iran, then swung between gains and losses throughout Wednesday.

New analysis released by Moody's Analytics chief economist Mark Zandi estimated the odds of the coronavirus turning into a pandemic were now at 40 percent—a development that Zandi said would result in a recession in the US for the first half of 2020.

"The coronavirus has been a body blow to the Chinese economy, which now threatens to take out the entire global economy," he wrote in a research note. "A global recession is likely if COVID-19 becomes a pandemic, and the odds of that are uncomfortably high."

The White House is also trying to work with leaders at the state level on a possible coronavirus response.

"There are nuances of the messaging that may lead some to believe we're saying something different," said Michael Kilkenny, medical director for the Cabell-Huntington Health Department in Huntington, W.Va. "But we all have the same understanding that this is a serious threat to the public health of the US, and that when we talk about a disease that has the potential to spread asymptomatically, the reality is you cannot stop community spread."

Kilkenny and other state and local health leaders met with administration officials including acting chief of staff Mick Mulvaney at the White House on Tuesday to discuss preparedness efforts for the coronavirus. He said he agreed with the CDC's assessment that community spread is likely.

"That's the prudent concept to grasp, and we're grasping that at the local levels across the country," Kilkenny said. "To deny that would happen here would be foolish."

QAnon Conspiracy Theories Fight Against Science

Marc-André Argentino

Marc-André Argentino is working toward a PhD at Concordia University in Montreal. He specializes in how religious extremist and political organizations create propaganda and recruit members.

First there was the pandemic, then came the "infodemic"—a term the head of the World Health Organization defines as the spread of false information about COVID-19.

The most dangerous conspiracy theories about the coronavirus are now part of the QAnon phenomenon. For months now, actors in QAnon have downplayed the severity of the crisis, amplified medical disinformation and have been originators of hoaxes.

The QAnon movement started in 2017 after someone using an anonymous account known only as Q posted wild conspiracy theories about US President Donald Trump on the internet forum 4chan.

QAnon conspiracy theorists believe a deep state cabal of global elites is responsible for all the evil in the world. They also believe those same elites are seeking to bring down Trump, whom they see as the world's only hope to defeat the deep state. QAnon has now brought the same conspiracy mentality to the coronavirus crisis.

As a researcher of online movements like QAnon, I use a combination of data science and digital ethnography to research how extremist movements use technology to create propaganda, recruit members to ideological causes, inspire acts of violence or impact democratic institutions.

"QAnon Conspiracy Theories About the Coronavirus Pandemic Are a Public Health Threat," by Marc-André Argentino, The Conversation, April 8, 2020. https:// theconversation.com/qanon-conspiracy-theories-about-the-coronavirus-pandemic-are-a -public-health-threat-135515. Licensed under CC BY-ND 4.0 International.

Bottom-Up Approach

A central component of QAnon is the crowdsourcing of narratives. This bottom-up approach provides a fluid and ever changing ideology. My analysis of Twitter shows from January to March, there was a 21 per cent increase (a total of 7,683,414 posts) in hashtags used by the QAnon community. This means the misinformation they spread has the capacity to reach a wider audience.

For instance, QAnon community influencers on Twitter promoted Miracle Mineral Supplement as a way of preventing COVID-19. The toxic product was sold by the Texas-based Genesis II Church of Health and Healing for US$45. The US Food and Drug Administration had previously issued a warning about the dangerous and potentially life threatening side effects of the supplement.

In January, QAnon was amplifying narratives on 8kun (the internet forum formally known as 8chan), Facebook and Telegram (an encrypted instant messaging plaform) about a false theory that Asians were more susceptible to the coronavirus and that white people were immune to COVID-19. Not only are there racist undertones associated with this disinformation, it minimizes the threat posed by the virus.

Downplayed Threat

From February until the second week of March, QAnon followed the lead of Trump in downplaying the threat of the virus and calling it a hoax. They believed the virus was a deep state plot to damage the president's chance at re-election. The QAnon community said those warning about the pandemic threat were trying to detract from US domestic politics, stop Trump rallies and remove all the economic gains they contended had occurred during the Trump presidency.

After the WHO upgraded COVID-19 to pandemic status and the US announced it was closing its borders to most people from Europe for 30 days, QAnon changed the narrative again. Suddenly,

QAnon thought the pandemic was something to celebrate because it was a cover for the Trump administration's secret plan to arrest deep state agents.

Evangelicals within the the QAnon movement viewed the pandemic as the promised coming of the Kingdom of God on Earth. David Hayes, who is better known as the Praying Medic and an influencer in the QAnon community with 300,000 YouTube subscribers, said in a March 14 livestream that there was no reason to be concerned about COVID-19. Hayes reassured his viewers that they may not be affected by the disease because this was "spiritual warfare"—only those who have not been chosen by God will be affected by the disease.

The person known as Q, who spawned the QAnon movement, didn't post anything online about COVID-19 until March 23. Up until then, all of the medical disinformation, hoaxes and downplaying of the pandemic had been sourced from QAnon influencers and community.

Public Health Threat

In his first post on the topic of COVID-19, Q pushed a conspiracy theory with racial undertones about COVID-19 being a Chinese bioweapon and that the virus release was a joint venture between China and the Democrats to stop Trump's re-election by destroying the economy.

The QAnon conspiracies have created an environment of complacency among its followers who aren't taking the risks posed by the virus seriously.

Florida pastor Rodney Howard-Browne, who has given credence to QAnon in the past and has preached that the coronavirus was planned by the Bill and Melinda Gates Foundation, was arrested after holding Sunday services and disregarding federal, state and county orders to limit gatherings to less than 10 people. His conspiratorial beliefs led to his negligent actions, which put hundreds of people from his congregation at risk.

In another instance, right-wing media figures were spreading an "empty hospital" conspiracy, downplaying the pandemic and its death toll.

A QAnon account originally launched the #FilmYourHospital hashtag. This was amplified by QAnon influencers such as former California congressional candidate DeAnna Lorraine Tesoriero and QAnon influencer Liz Crokin. This hoax was then picked up by mainstream right-wing media figures promoting COVID trutherism to a wider audience.

The FBI once called conspiracy theories spread by QAnon and others a "potential domestic terrorism threat." It's time to call the infodemic a public health threat.

The Science-Policy Interface Can Be Improved by Integrating Scientific Investigation with Political Debate

Peter Horton and Garrett W. Brown

Peter Horton is affiliated with the Grantham Centre for Sustainable Futures and Department of Molecular Biology and Biotechnology, University of Sheffield. Garrett W. Brown is affiliated with the School of Politics and International Studies, University of Leeds.

There is currently intense debate over expertise, evidence and "post-truth" politics, and how this is influencing policy formulation and implementation. In this article, we put forward a methodology for evidence-based policy making intended as a way of helping navigate this web of complexity. Starting from the premise of why it is so crucial that policies to meet major global challenges use scientific evidence, we discuss the socio-political difficulties and complexities that hinder this process. We discuss the necessity of embracing a broader view of what constitutes evidence—science and the evaluation of scientific evidence cannot be divorced from the political, cultural and social debate that inevitably and justifiably surrounds these major issues. As a pre-requisite for effective policy making, we propose a methodology that fully integrates scientific investigation with political debate and social discourse. We describe a rigorous process of mapping, analysis, visualisation and sharing of evidence, constructed from integrating science and social science data. This would then be followed by transparent evidence evaluation, combining independent assessment to test the validity and completeness of the evidence with deliberation to discover how the evidence is perceived, misunderstood or ignored. We outline the opportunities

"Integrating Evidence, Politics and Society: A Methodology for the Science-Policy Interface," by Peter Horton and Garrett W. Brown, Palgrave Commun 4, 42 (2018). https://doi.org/10.1057/s41599-018-0099-3. Licensed under CC BY-4.0 International.

and the problems derived from the use of digital communications, including social media, in this methodology, and emphasise the power of creative and innovative evidence visualisation and sharing in shaping policy.

Introduction

As the world struggles with complex problems that affect all aspects of human civilisation—from climate change and loss of ecosystems and biodiversity, to overpopulation, malnutrition and poverty, to disease, ill health and an ageing population—never before has it been more important to base government policy for intervention upon scientific evidence. In this article, we outline a methodology for integrating the process of scientific investigation with political debate and social discourse in order to improve the science-policy interface.

Science advisors and advisory bodies with scientist representation have steadily increased (Gluckman and Wilsdon, 2016); for example, in the UK in the form of the Food Standard Agency (FSA), the Human Fertilisation and Embryology Authority (HFEA) and the National Institute for Health and Care Excellence (NICE) or globally within the commissions and advisory bodies associated with the United Nations and/or the use of technical review panels such as within The Global Fund to Fight Aids, Malaria and Tuberculosis. The well-established Intergovernmental Panel on Climate Change (IPCC) is a model for other panels, such as the Intergovernmental Platform on Biodiversity and Ecosystem Services. However, the process by which scientific evidence becomes part of a policy is complicated and messy (Gluckman, 2017; Malakoff, 2017), and there are many examples to support the view that this results in fundamental failings to deal quickly or effectively with major global challenges. For example, the time lag between the beginning of meaningful climate action in the COP21 Paris Agreement and the science that proved that greenhouse gas emissions are changing the climate illustrates the difficulty of evidence-based policy making. It also questions the ultimate effectiveness of policy making, since there is evidence to suggest that COP21 may be too little, too late (Rockstrom et al., 2017). Similarly, the continued EU embargo on the use of food from genetically modified (GM) crops shows a serious disconnect between public opinion and the huge amount of scientific evidence that shows that the environmental and health risks are infinitesimal.

What Is Evidence?

The reasons for these apparent failures are complicated and numerous but one key issue is what constitutes evidence. Even when the problem is clearly one where science can provide a solution, evidence is not only derived from scientific investigation, but also from the political, cultural, economic and social dimensions of these issues, resulting in arguments about relative validity and worth. Hence, bias and prejudice are difficult to remove and evidence is often cherry-picked, only lightly consulted, partially worked into policy (if at all), and/or side-stepped in favour of ideological preferences. Even when evidence is abundant and clear, it is often ignored as we enter a "post-truth" era where the opinions of experts are viewed with scepticism and populist solutions predominate (e.g., a 140 character tweet can brand a piece of sound scientific evidence as "fake news"). The ready availability and sharing of information through the internet and social media, which in some sense democratise evidence by increasing the diversity of inputs, should be a positive and welcome development. Condorcet's mathematical Jury Theorem suggests that "larger groups make better decisions" and that more, and diverse, input leads to better "collective intelligence" (Condorcet, 1785). Thus, the increase in diverse information should foster "the wisdom of crowds" (Surowiecki, 2005) towards "the better argument" (Landemore and Elster, 2012). However, online content is personalised through the use of algorithms aimed to harvest and respond to existing preferences. Thus, the internet often fosters an "echo chamber" effect that limits cognitive diversity and increases "group think" by providing and linking information based solely on the entrenched preferences of the internet user and like-minded individuals (Grassegger and Krogerus, 2016). In addition, there is a view that scientific investigation is not clear, takes place outside the public sphere and often perceived as purposefully elitist. This gives rise to conspiracies about who produced the evidence and for what purpose, eroding epistemic authority. As a result, highly personalised preferences are reinforced by selective information, despite the fact that this information might amount to misinformation, exaggeration, falsehood and degraded or "cherry-picked" evidence. Hence, rational policy development is thwarted because governments are tempted to use the evidence that concurs with the preconceived views of their constituents as well as their own existing political mantras, or which confirms public perceptions and aspirations, whether this mirrors the best available evidence or not.

The Problem with Scientific Evidence

For scientists this is a particularly difficult problem to deal with. Science establishes facts, such as the fundamental physics proving that increasing levels of CO2 in the atmosphere will result in an increased greenhouse effect. Even when proof is elusive (such as knowing exactly how, where and when this greenhouse effect will be translated into changes in climate) the notion of evidence is sacrosanct, it being derived from objective analysis, evaluation, testing, experimentation, retesting and falsifiability. To see hard won evidence ignored, distorted or diluted in favour of what seem ill-informed subjective views leads to frustration and anger. However, a more constructive and positive response would be to realise that the evaluation of scientific evidence cannot be divorced from the political, cultural and social debate that inevitably and justifiably surrounds most major issues. Using the two examples above, the long and sometimes tortuous pathway to the COP21 climate change accord results from the difficult economic trade-offs involved and the very different socio-political perspectives of the nations of the world. In the case of GM, the emotional context of food consumption that may favour natural foods cannot be treated dismissively, nor can the legitimate concerns about increased power and control that GM might give to multinational agri-businesses. As stated elsewhere (Cairney, 2016), scientific investigation defines problems, but often does not identify policy-acceptable, scalable and meaningful solutions. Scientists are often not effective in communicating their findings to audiences outside academia and frequently hold naive assumptions that good evidence will be readily accepted and can quickly contribute to policy. Not appreciating the complexity and non-linearity of many of the intractable problems that science is addressing (so-called wicked problems—DeFries and Nagendra, 2017) is often the root cause of this failure. Thus, the question often asked is can we improve the ways in which scientific evidence is constructed, integrated and communicated, so it can contribute more effectively, efficiently and quickly into policy formulation, in ways that combat the problems of a "post-truth" era.

Producing Evidence

Ideas for a policy intervention follow identification of a particular societal problem and may be initiated by a variety of organisations—governments, agencies of government such as research funding bodies, political parties, pressure groups, NGOs, think-tanks or groups of concerned academics. It may be top-down or bottom-up. This is then followed by the production of evidence about the operation, implementation and effectiveness of the policy idea, commissioned or carried out by the policy proposer. The process of evidence production normally follows a number of steps [such] as a MAVS cycle—an iterative process of mapping, analysis, visualisation and sharing (Horton et al., 2016).

The usefulness of formalising evidence generation in this way was demonstrated in addressing a specific policy question of how to reduce the environmental impact of the production of bread (Goucher et al., 2017; Horton, 2017). Mapping identified all the key actors in the wheat-bread supply chain, from whom data was obtained. This complete data set was then analysed by a standardised process of Life Cycle Assessment. The evidence clearly showed the dominant contribution of fertiliser as a source of greenhouse gas emissions—which was presented in easily visualised form, and shared via publication in a peer-reviewed academic journal (Goucher et al., 2017), press releases and a summary article in The Conversation (Horton, 2017). These were widely read and discussed across a wide variety of media. The evidence was subsequently taken up by commercial bodies in the wheat-bread industry who are now seeking ways towards a "sustainable bread."

We suggest that the MAVS methodology could be similarly useful in evidence gathering for many other policy purposes. In such cases the evidence might be much more complex than in the above example, because policy more often than not is addressing complex multidimensional wicked problems rather than purely technical ones. One challenge is how to integrate scientific evidence, which is usually quantitative data, with the qualitative data obtained by social sciences. For this, further development of social indicators is crucial, including indicators of well-being, values, agency and inequality (Hicks et al., 2016). Furthermore, what is being suggested here is that evidence production should not be limited to only presenting analytically coherent statements about "facts," "truth" and "solutions." Thus, evidence also needs to be generated in direct response to existing preferences as a means to either support or falsify preferences in a way that speaks to them, not over them. Here, interdisciplinary incorporation of social science techniques adds to the scientific data by providing stakeholder analysis, preference identification and social categorisation.

Lessons could be learned from recent experiments aimed to increase health policy outcomes associated with the production of evidence by means of participatory research models, which incorporate stakeholders into the design (mapping), evaluation (analysis), communication (visualisation and sharing) and implementation phases of research. By doing so, several unique features result. Firstly, stakeholders are able to provide "on the ground" insights about the problems or misunderstandings the research needs to address. Hence the research questions are tailored to these needs and the final aims of the research made transparent. Secondly, by including stakeholders throughout the process, it creates "buy-in" and better understanding of how the evidence was created, increasing epistemic authority while undermining conspiratory speculation and claims of elitism. Thirdly, inclusion naturally builds trust in the results, which in many cases in health research has allowed for better policy translation and outcomes, since people are more willing to adopt the rationale for a policy if they feel that they were involved in the process. As an example, positive policy results have been witnessed in a number of cases where health research linked circumcision to reduced rates of HIV infection in Africa. Although it is still a highly contentious issue in many parts of the world, the inclusion of political, religious and cultural leaders in the research process in many cases helped to alleviate existing fears and misunderstandings, which facilitated more exact communication and acceptance of the source of evidence (WHO, 2016).

Visualisation and sharing are particularly important steps of the MAVS process. All too often, evidence production and analysis results in lengthy and often impenetrable reports, which make the process of transparent evidence sharing impossible and often counter-productive. For example, Howarth and Painter (2016) describe the problems translating the information contained in IPCC reports into local action plans. Thus, research is urgently needed to find the best ways to visualise and then communicate evidence, for example, using clever infographics and other digital techniques. There is huge potential for evidence sharing via web-based national and international events and new online publishing models (e.g., Horton, 2017). Most important of all, people with expert knowledge need to be active and pro-active rather than passive and reactive; indeed one might argue they have a responsibility to do so. Jeremy Grantham, founder of the philanthropic Grantham Foundation for the Protection of the

Environment once stated, "Be persuasive. Be brave. Be arrested (if necessary)" (Grantham, 2012). Sharing of experience and approaches is also vital, to find out what works and what doesn't, creating networks if appropriate, such as the International Network of Government Science Advice (INGSA) or less formal and spontaneous movements such as that which resulted in the March for Science. Supplementing evidence with powerful stories from "real life" can also increase the effectiveness of communication. One key implication here is that what may previously have been regarded as research (in a university for example) may become an activity in which the end result, in terms of impact, advocacy and implementation, is not just an optional "add-on" but an integral and obligatory part of the project.

Evaluating Evidence

The next step in our methodology is evidence evaluation. This is an open and transparent process that questions the validity of the evidence. Who leads this evaluation process will depend upon who is leading the policy initiative. Given their reputation for impartiality, transparency and interdisciplinary thinking, universities could play a key independent role, so long as they have procedures to include all stakeholders, particularly those directly affected by a policy intervention. This is not always straightforward, especially when research depends upon funding by governments and various external bodies. The key is to break away from the traditional model of the "expert panel of mostly white male senior academics" and strive towards diversity of experience, ethnicity and gender. Again, the criterion for such assessment is not to produce an impenetrable report, but to follow the principles of visualisation and sharing set out above.

Evidence evaluation simultaneously and equally combines discussion, debate and deliberation with testing of that evidence in further independent scientific scrutiny, including using peer review procedures well known for academic science. Evidence from scientific investigation rarely constitutes proof and furthermore does not always meet high standards of objectivity, quality or neutrality. Therefore, it has to be independently assessed, including by consideration of evidence available from other sources and studies. Within the evaluation process it is important to locate not only where evidence is lacking or is inconclusive or ambiguous, but also to understand how evidence is perceived, misunderstood or ignored. Thus, for example, the same piece of evidence can be interpreted in different ways by different stakeholders, leading to disagreement and conflict (discussed in Horton et al., 2016). These then become focal points in deliberative forums that consider the tension between different actors and stakeholders.

The use of stakeholder deliberative forums within the evidence policy process not only allows for misconceptions and ideological stances to be located and understood, but also provides deliberative opportunities for various ideological positions to be held to public scrutiny by other stakeholders. Stakeholders with particularly entrenched preferences are asked to share these preferences and give their best defences and evidence to support them. This includes having stakeholder positions tested against the best evidence available and mutual requests of reason giving from other stakeholders. Deliberative forums help to undermine enclave thinking and force ideology testing via the need for public reason giving. They have had empirical success in creating intersubjective meta-understandings between stakeholders, which over time, allow crucial agreements on key factual elements within contested public policy.

There are already many cases of governments instituting deliberative forums for key policy discussions, in efforts to generate policy consensus, rather than relying on aggregative preference tallying models that only measure existing preferences and pit them against each other in simplistic minority/majority binaries. For example, there have been successful deliberative experiments trialled by the Western Australian Department of Planning and Infrastructure, in British Columbia's "Citizens Assembly," in Ireland during the Irish Constitutional Convention, and by Oregon State in its "Initiative Review" (Rosenberg, 2007).

Although deliberative forums have largely been physical meetings facilitated by researchers, governments or experts, the use of the internet to broaden the scope of deliberative forums could hold promising innovation. This could allow much wider participation and larger sets of data to be collected and evaluated, aided by the use of artificial intelligence techniques. This is an area to which future research should be directed (Neblo et al., 2017).

Transforming Knowledge into Policy

The results of this two-pronged evaluation are viewed together in the process by which the evidence associated with a policy idea is transformed into a policy plan. The policy plan can then be evaluated again, and again, step-by-step until all evidence has been validated and all stakeholder viewpoints have been reasonably satisfied or properly discredited. The policy is then ready for implementation. The anticipation here is that stakeholder "buy-in" will remove barriers to policy implementation and that the use of evidence within these deliberations shape that "buy-in." This is because, although politicians could still ignore evidence-based policy consensus, they would have less incentive to do so if that consensus demonstrated a clear "buy-in" by key stakeholders and the public. In addition, deliberative forums often involve policy makers as key participants and thus can deliver preference alteration, particularly if they are aligned at the same time as other constituent stakeholders.

Can the methodology we describe have an effect on the development of evidence-based policy in general? Combining scientific analysis, participation and deliberation among multiple stakeholders, has been proposed to address the problem of water sustainability (Garrick et al., 2017), food security (Horton et al., 2017) and health (Lucero et al., 2018), and it is in such domains that we foresee it being particularly applicable. However, in many cases the full complexity and messiness of the problem may make strict adherence to this methodology difficult, and here evidence sharing through advocacy, stakeholder outreach and campaigning becomes particularly important. Politicians often take note only when public pressure mounts, for example, because of intense activity in the popular press, as in the recent policy proposals in the UK surrounding plastic bottles, coffee cups and plastic pollution of the oceans. It is perhaps less clear whether our methodology can make impact in more politically charged policy areas such as climate change, where evidence is clear but vested interests, often through "post-truth" and "fake news" work to undermine it. Nevertheless, having a formal framework could be a source of stability, discipline and confidence building, a recourse when problems arise and a way to break through log jams and overcome barriers. By establishing trust between scientists, government and the public, it could help build a more effective science-policy interface.

Waiving Intellectual Property Protections Is Key to Fighting the Pandemic Around the World

Daniel Takash

Daniel Takash is a regulatory policy fellow at the Niskanen Center. He researches regulatory policies on occupational licensing, financialization, land use regulation and zoning, intellectual property, and other topics related to regressive rent-seeking.

Yesterday, United States Trade Representative Katherine Tai announced that the Biden Administration would support waiving intellectual property enforcement requirements under the Agreement Trade-Related Aspects of Intellectual Property Rights (TRIPS):

> This is a global health crisis, and the extraordinary circumstances of the COVID-19 pandemic call for extraordinary measures. The Administration believes strongly in intellectual property protections, but in service of ending this pandemic, supports the waiver of those protections for COVID-19 vaccines. We will actively participate in text-based negotiations at the World Trade Organization (WTO) needed to make that happen. Those negotiations will take time given the consensus-based nature of the institution and the complexity of the issues involved.
>
> The Administration's aim is to get as many safe and effective vaccines to as many people as fast as possible. As our vaccine supply for the American people is secured, the Administration will continue to ramp up its efforts—working with the private sector and all possible partners—to expand vaccine manufacturing and distribution. It will also work to increase the raw materials needed to produce those vaccines.

Last week, President Biden announced plans to ship 60 million doses of the AstraZeneca vaccine and the materials required to India, which is currently facing one of the deadliest COVID-19 outbreaks of the pandemic. The United States' support for the waiver will supercharge the fight against the pandemic across the world.

First introduced in October 2020, a pending resolution at the World Trade Organization (WTO) brought by South Africa and India would waive requirements for member states to enforce most intellectual property rights during the COVID-19 pandemic. A growing number of legislators in the United States have joined the countless activists, world leaders, public interest organizations calling for the US to support the waiver. If passed by the WTO, it would be an effective tool to help countries bring their COVID-19 outbreaks under control by unleashing the drug manufacturing capacity of nations outside the US. The Niskanen Center is gratified that the Administration has officially joined their ranks and supports the relaxation of regulations that restrict vaccine supply and development.

"This is spectacular news, but it's only the first step," said Daniel Takash, Regulatory Policy Fellow at the Niskanen Center. "President Biden has made some comments about the sharing of "know-how" necessary to make vaccines, which goes well beyond intellectual property. Not only does this cover trade secrets and copyright restrictions, it includes the sharing of unprotectable skills and knowledge that will require active measures from the public and private sector to make them widely available. Unlike the waiver, which is simply the removal of a barrier to access, this would require active measures by the US and other governments for which no expense should be spared. Between previous comments made by President Biden and yesterday's announcement, I'm extremely optimistic about the potential for a Marshall Plan for technology transfer."

"Vaccine manufacturing can't turn on a dime and technology transfers don't happen overnight, but they are effective and will remove some of the supply-side constraints on vaccine production," said Takash. "But these same time constraints apply to vaccine distribution, with some saying that global herd immunity may not occur by 2022 or even 2024. Every day people across the world aren't vaccinated leads to more death and more opportunities for the virus to mutate, making time of the essence."

This double-barrelled approach is essential, as technology transfers will provide India's well-established pharmaceutical industry with the expertise needed to manufacture vaccines at scale. But intellectual property on the drugs themselves is only part of the equation. "Access to academic literature needed by frontline healthcare professionals and researchers alike is kept behind high paywalls and restrictions on 'data mining' and other methods of data analysis," says Takash. "The legal risks associated with running afoul of intellectual property restrictions are myriad, and the TRIPS waiver will remove the legal Sword of Damocles threatening those who can contribute far more in fighting COVID than they are allowed to do."

The world's largest democracy has stepped up to the plate in the past. During the HIV/AIDS crisis, Indian drug manufacturers contributed the lion's share of affordable drugs to the developing world while brand-name manufacturers hoarded knowledge and kept prices for these life-saving drugs at prices beyond reach to those who needed them most. It's time for the United States and the rest of the world to return the favor, and Ambassador Tai's announcement is a major part of that.

Science Diplomats Can Facilitate Multilateral Responses to Global Challenges

Lorenzo Melchor

Lorenzo Melchor works as European Union science advice and diplomacy officer in the Spanish Foundation for Science and Technology. He holds a PhD in molecular biology and has had an international academic career in cancer genetics for thirteen years in Spain, the United States, and the United Kingdom, with over 30 academic peer-reviewed publications.

Although an intense international scientific collaboration has occurred to tackle the pandemic, national governments have failed in co-ordinating an immediate multilateral response. This global challenge has brought the interface between science, policy and diplomacy to the spotlight, with science informing governments and facilitating diplomatic collaborations. However, different interface frictions, system deficiencies and stoppers have hindered a science diplomacy–based multilateral response that could have ameliorated this situation. This has occurred even with the field of science diplomacy (SD) receiving bigger attention since the Barack Obama administration's new diplomacy approach in the Middle East and the seminal conference by the Royal Society of London and the American Association for the Advancement of Science (AAAS) in 2009. The European Union has also contributed, with Commissioner Carlos Moedas implementing SD as an important dimension in his Open to the World policy. Yet the concrete meaning of SD and the nature of the wide range of practitioners involved remain elusive. Hence, two questions follow.

First, what is science diplomacy? There are different SD conceptualisations, with the Madrid Declaration on Science

"What Is a Science Diplomat?" by Lorenzo Melchor, *Hague Journal of Diplomacy*, August 10, 2020, https://brill.com/view/journals/hjd/15/3/article-p409_11 .xml?language=en. Licensed under CC BY-4.0 International.

Diplomacy describing it as "a series of practices at the intersection of science, technology and foreign policy." SD is a transboundary field sitting across: 1) national borders, entailing bilateral or multilateral relationships; 2) policy frameworks, combining the policy realms of science, technology, innovation and foreign affairs—each with clear-cut definitions of competencies, actors and levels—and establishing complex and fluid interactions with joint jurisdictions; 3) stakeholders of all natures, involving government actors as well as international organisations, scientific institutions, non-governmental organisations (NGOs), the private sector and so forth; and 4) professional backgrounds, because it bridges two cultures with different world views: the scientist and the diplomat.

[…]

The Science Diplomat: Definition and Taxonomy

SD is a complex space where professionals with different backgrounds gather to build collaborations and potentially seek common interests. On one side are scientists who may be active researchers taking some responsibilities as advisers or diplomats to build international partnerships and influence or represent their nation's interest (the diplomat scientist); on the other are diplomats who have specialised in science, technology and innovation (STI) affairs (the scientist diplomat). These are two well-defined professions that sporadically, or for a certain time, may take responsibilities in addition to their traditional ones (e.g., conducting research and innovation in the case of scientists; representing their country, defending national interests, supporting expatriates and building international relationships following the Vienna Convention on Diplomatic Relations (1961) in the case of diplomats). A third figure comprises different actors—civil servants, embassy staff, science/policy managers, innovation delegates, liaison officers, policy scientists and so forth—whose professional task is mediating between science and diplomacy, providing support to the aforementioned figures or even leading/

implementing their own actions and institutional strategies. These professionals have become full-time SD specialists.

Science diplomats could be widely defined as professionals— be they scientists or diplomats—who work to place STI affairs as an important dimension within international relations and the international policy system. Because SD transcends international scientific co-operation, science diplomats not only connect scientists working in different countries to establish collaborations, but especially strive to connect scientists with diplomats, government officials and political leaders to raise the presence and influence of STI in international affairs.

SD occurs in diverse contexts with extensive variation between countries and institutions about how individuals get recruited or trained to fulfil SD roles, how their career paths are envisioned and what political relevance is attributed to their specific area.

[...]

The Science Diplomat's Toolbox

SD approaches and conceptual understandings differ between scientists and diplomats. Two different cultures with distinguishable and sometimes opposing philosophies, interests, values and mind sets meet in this interface.

The set of required knowledge and skills to perform as science diplomats who bring both worlds together is quite broad. Depending on their backgrounds, they need to develop a specific subset. Broadly, science diplomats need to know how scientific research is conducted and have a basic understanding of the national/international STI landscapes to better engage with the scientific community. Also, they need to be familiar with policy affairs and international relationships to understand the setting in which they are working. They need to nurture skills in communication, negotiation, management, intercultural sensitivity, networking, storytelling, languages, science literacy and much more.

Challenges

After reviewing what a science diplomat is and the required skills, some readers may be or would like to be science diplomats working in institutionalised positions but they should be aware of certain challenges.

First, SD has no clear career path, as many different positions do not necessarily state "science diplomacy" in their names. When recalling their own personal voyages, science diplomats with scientific backgrounds often share their exposure to policy environments through life-transforming events such as those involving policy fellowship schemes, expeditions and international summits. Networking in policy environments and engaging with potential mentors can prove useful for better understanding your interests and where you can best fit in.

Second, scientists are not usually trained in international law, diplomacy, public administration, governance or policy-making. Taking another master's or executive programme to get formal education may be useful for understanding the world you are stepping into.

Third, institutionalised positions may operate between two government departments. This is a delicate position as you may need to combine separate interests and understandings, and navigate potential frictions.

Fourth, do not expect that you will be heard and be influential from day zero. Building trust and your own reputation takes time, hard work, establishing fruitful collaborations, arranging meetings with the scientific community and respecting chains of command.

Fifth, scientists tend to be more negative about SD than diplomats. Scientists may mistrust SD practices and professionals because of the risk of manipulation of science for political gain; the lack of immediate research career incentives if involved in SD; the impression that SD does not provide instant improvements in national STI systems, research funding or researchers' career conditions; or the fact that leaving behind an academic career may still be perceived as a failure. Conversely, diplomats welcome these interface professionals as they help them gain access to scientific knowledge and contacts.

Recommendations

As someone trained as a scientist who has worked at an embassy, the author puts forward the following recommendations to current and potential science diplomats, who may adapt them to their specific context:

It is a figure-it-out position within a team! There is no manual of instructions to read when you start working in SD. You need to realise what is expected from you and have an entrepreneurial and proactive attitude (e.g., design an innovative programme never before tried in your institution). Speak with your colleagues in other destinations and engage with your government headquarters to share best practices and conceive common strategies.

Science is just one piece in the puzzle but try to embed it everywhere! In diplomacy, there are different interests at play and science is just one of many. Sometimes you will be frustrated when your advice or project is not followed or approved due to other interests. Learn from the experience to better understand the whole picture and how science fits in it, and to improve your persuasion skills for future opportunities. Also, consider how to connect the embassy departments (trade, economy, education, transportation, agriculture, culture) with the scientific community to raise the importance of science in their portfolios (e.g., arranging joint events or meetings with scientific experts). Finally, try to import scientific practices (e.g., critical thinking, peer-review) to your current setting as they may improve established processes and policy-making.

Identify your foreign counterparts for bilateral and multilateral synergies! You work in an international setting for bringing countries together. Monitor the latest breakthroughs in research and science policy in your destination country and explore collaboration opportunities between governments (STI bilateral agreements, joint research funds, science governance practice exchange). Make sure you defend your national interests while being as open and collaborative as possible with your foreign counterparts. Also, engage with the thriving global community of science diplomats to learn from others, publish in specialised journals and seek synergies.

Be humble, communicative, trustworthy and keep your eyes open! Be humble when approaching other professionals, as they may be open for collaboration or know of someone who shares your interest. Use common language that avoids jargon and improve your narrative skills to leave behind scholarly explanations. Build your trust and reputation to enhance the image of your institution by keeping in contact with your network and making anyone feel part of your successes; the smart use of social media can help you. Finally, read and watch the news because a constant flow of issues merits your attention at an embassy; you never know when your advice or action could effect a change.

Involve the general public! This should not be a dialogue exclusively between scientists and diplomats, when populisms, pseudoscience, fake news and citizen mistrust of experts and democratic institutions seem to be on the rise. Involving citizens in your activities will expose them to how scientific knowledge and democratic institutions both operate. Consider their feedback, too, as new research opportunities and improvements in institutional settings may arise from this.

Conclusion

With the growing importance of STI affairs in diplomacy and the emergence of global challenges, nation states require more science diplomats in institutionalised and non-institutionalised positions. These professionals are key to preserving national interests that ensure socio-economic competitiveness but also facilitate multilateral responses for addressing global challenges.

CHAPTER 3

Does Politics Influence Medical Treatment During a Pandemic?

Overview: The COVID-19 Pandemic Underscored the Inequities in Healthcare

N. Jensen, A. H. Kelly, and M. Avendano

N. Jensen, A. H. Kelly, and M. Avendano are affiliated with the Department of Global Health and Social Medicine, King's College London.

COVID-19 has ravaged health systems and economies in countries across the world. While many would argue that a pandemic of respiratory disease was predictable, the systematic failures of the response came as a surprise. From the shortage of hospital beds and medical equipment to the gross insufficiencies in national surveillance systems, supply chains and laboratory capacity, COVID-19 has laid bare the health care limitations that "global north" and "global south" share. A stark set of differences, however, run across the parallels in our collective predicament: indeed, what has become ever-more apparent is the radically uneven distribution of the health, social and economic risks associated with the pandemic—and the public health measures implemented in response—both within and between societies. As concerns grow over a prolonged period of COVID-19 waves, further insights are needed into who bears the largest share of COVID-19 burden and why. The pursuit of health equity is widely held to be global health's raison d'être; and yet, the deep inequities laid bare by the current pandemic underscore that the field must do more and we must do better.

[...]

"The COVID-19 Pandemic Underscores the Need for an Equity-Focused Global Health Agenda," by N. Jensen, A. H. Kelly, and M. Avendano. *Humanities and Social Sciences Communications,* January 18, 2021. https://www.nature.com/articles/s41599-020-00700 -x#Sec1. Licensed under CC BY-4.0 International.

COVID-19 as a Magnifier of Health Inequalities

As the pandemic evolved, perhaps the most striking finding has been the disproportionally high infection and mortality rates among people from Black and Minority Ethnic (BAME) backgrounds in the UK (Public Health England, 2020) and among African Americans (CDC, 2020). The impact of the pandemic is also clearly gendered: although men generally appear more vulnerable to COVID-19 infection, women make up the majority of the global health workforce at increased risk of hospital infection (Wenham et al., 2020).

[...]

As much as the pandemic points to the dangers of imposing "one-size-fits-all" public health approaches in vastly different contexts (Mehtar et al., 2020; Cash and Patel, 2020), it also highlights that no rapidly implemented emergency response mechanism can offset the structural fragilities of healthcare and social welfare benefit systems caused by decades of underinvestment and neglect.

That well-functioning healthcare systems are key to achieving health equity has become a truism in high-level global health debates, consolidated over the past two decades around the push for Health System Strengthening (HSS). Within these discussions, poorer countries' health systems tend to be portrayed as "bottlenecks" to the delivery of evidence-based healthcare services. To many, the calamitous effects COVID-19 on "weak" health systems, especially in Africa, seemed inevitable.

In many African nations Covid-19 has indeed exposed severe constraints in terms of testing and surveillance capacities, numbers of health workers, Personal Protective Equipment (PPE) stockpiles, intensive care unit (ICU) beds, ventilation systems and constrained health budgets to scale up outbreak responses (Nkengasong and Mankoula, 2020). The clarity with which those limitations have been brought into view have the potential to springboard internationally supported HSS efforts to the forefront of global health policy. In some key ways, however, the pandemic has also exposed the ways in which the current HSS agenda falls short.

First, the breadth of country responses to the pandemic has highlighted examples of less-resourced countries that have launched effective public health measures to mitigate the impact of COVID-19 on their often fragile health systems (Dalglish, 2020). But, conversely, the pandemic has also exposed that health and social care system constraints are by no means limited to poorer "global south" countries. Governments across the world have struggled to robustly respond to growing infection rates with medical and public health infrastructures that have been weakened by years of underinvestment, reorganisation and fragmentation. This holds true, for example, for the US, where the outgoing administration stifled implementation of the 2010 Affordable Care Act (ACA), which many had hoped would alleviate glaring health disparities by improving healthcare access especially for ethnic minorities and socio-economically disadvantaged groups (Williams et al., 2016; van Dorn et al., 2020; Himmelstein and Woolhandler, 2020). In the UK and many continental European countries, a twin drive towards cost reduction and privatisation has hollowed out health systems over at least the past decade, with indications that it is the health of poor and marginalised populations that has suffered most as a result (Karanikolos et al., 2013; Stuckler et al., 2017; McCoy, 2020).

Second, the current pandemic has revealed that health systems are rarely "weak" in isolation. As the International Labour Organization (ILO) notes, the COVID-19 pandemic has "revealed the cracks in social protection systems" (ILO, 2020). Indeed, despite improvements over the past decade, across many African countries, for example, coverage of social protection systems remains low, which risked rendering social distancing measures ineffective (Ebuenyi, 2020). But in many European countries, too, reduced or stagnating healthcare funding in the wake of the 2007–2008 financial crisis has often accompanied wider programmes of public sector cuts with often significant indirect health impacts: determinants of health such as unemployment, homelessness, food insecurity and mental health issues increased across many European countries linked to reduced government spending; at the same time that social protection programmes that may mitigate their impact on health were often scaled back (Thomson et al., 2015; Stuckler et al., 2017).

An acknowledgement that past policies have served to create global inequities and stifled countries' ability to respond to public health emergencies must be the first step towards transforming not just health but also social security systems. More so, it should make clear that the strive for health equity cannot be divorced from a wider agenda for social, economic and political justice. That comprehensive political commitment was central to the 1978 Alma Ata Declaration but has since been progressively watered down, including by the HSS agenda where this is used to promote a narrow path towards health equity via the provision of healthcare alone.

An equity approach would reaffirm these commitments by calling for interventions into the social, economic and political conditions that (re-)create inequities. As part of this, more clearly needs to be done to acknowledge and address those forms of injustice and oppression that are embedded within and articulated through sectors and institutions of public life, including those related to health and healthcare.

[…]

Conclusion

If anything, the current pandemic has been a powerful reminder that health is much more than just a medical matter, as it is embedded within a complex set of social, economic and political determinants. Providing a comprehensive picture of the overlapping, durational and socially situated burden of the pandemic will thus require a multi-disciplinary approach: next to epidemiological evidence that documents inequalities in outcomes and care, in depth qualitative and ethnographic research will be critical to evidence the heterogenous on-the-ground experiences and impacts of the pandemic, highlight the limitations and blindspots of one-size-fits-all pandemic responses, and point to the complex pathways through which imbalances in power and resources lead to health inequities.

The current crisis underscores why the pursuit of health equity should remain the top priority in global health. But it also lays bare the gap between the equity ambitions of the global health field and healthcare realities. The attention that the pandemic has brought to social and health inequalities may offer an opportunity to address that shortcoming. But, in so doing, it should also serve as a prompt to re-think the global health equity agenda and re-claim it is part of a much wider struggle for social, economic, political and epistemic justice.

Despite Warnings from Medical Experts, the President Touted Ineffective Treatments

The Hindu

The Hindu is the second-largest daily English language newspaper in India.

U S President Donald Trump has again defended the use of hydroxychloroquine to ward off coronavirus, saying many frontline medical workers agree with him that the malaria drug works in the early stages of COVID-19 infection, despite mounting evidence that it is ineffective in treating the disease.

In May, Mr. Trump disclosed that he was taking daily doses of hydroxychloroquine to ward off coronavirus after consulting the White House doctor.

"I happen to believe in it [hydroxychloroquine]. I would take it. As you know, I took it for a 14-day period, and I'm here. I happen to think it works in the early stages. I think frontline medical people believe that too—some, many," Mr. Trump told reporters at a White House news conference on July 28.

"But the one thing we know: It's been out for a long time, that particular formula, and that's essentially, what it is, the pill. And it's been for malaria, lupus, and other things. It's safe. It doesn't cause problems. I had no problem. I had absolutely no problem, felt no different. Didn't feel good, bad, or indifferent. I tested, as you know. It didn't hurt me, and it's not going to hopefully hurt anybody," he said.

There is no evidence that the drug can fight the virus, and regulators warn it may cause heart problems.

Last month, the US Food and Drug Administration (FDA) cautioned against the use of the drug for treatment of the coronavirus, following reports of "serious heart rhythm problems" and other health issues.

"US President Donald Trump Defends Use of Hydroxychloroquine, Says It Works in Early Stages of COVID-19 Infection," *The Hindu*, July 29, 2020. Reprinted by permission.

The World Health Organization (WHO) says "there is currently no proof" that it is effective as a treatment or prevents COVID-19.

"Many doctors think hydroxychloroquine is extremely successful: the hydroxychloroquine coupled with the zinc and perhaps the azithromycin. But many doctors think it's extremely good, and some people don't. I think it's become very political," Mr. Trump said referring to the controversy surrounding the malaria drug.

"We know from that standpoint—because it's been so many years, from a safety standpoint, it's safe. I happen to think, based on what I've read—I've read a lot about hydroxy. I happen to think that it has an impact, especially in the early years. There were some very good tests at Ford, and the doctor from Yale came up with a very, very strong testament to it," he said.

There are no FDA-approved drugs for the coronavirus, which has infected more than 16 million people worldwide and killed at least 655,300, according to data compiled by Johns Hopkins University.

More than 150,000 Americans have died because of coronavirus and over 4.4 million have tested positive.

Hydroxychloroquine sulfate was first synthesised in 1946 and is in a class of medications historically used to treat and prevent malaria. It is approved by the US Food and Drug Administration to treat malaria, rheumatoid arthritis, lupus, childhood arthritis, and other autoimmune diseases.

The drug generated excitement earlier in the year after small studies suggested it could be beneficial, especially when combined with antibiotic azithromycin. Mr. Trump promoted it as a potential treatment for the virus and said he used it as a preventive measure against the disease. However, several larger studies showed the drug was not helpful and caused heart issues in some patients.

The drug is not FDA-approved for the treatment of COVID-19 but it has been identified as a possible treatment for the infection and the US government has requested its immediate availability.

Science Denial Hampered the Pandemic Response

Adam Wernick

Adam Wernick is a freelance journalist for PRI.org.

S cience denial in the United States has for decades fueled resistance to taking action on climate change. As a consequence, the battle to prevent its worst effects may already be lost. That same science denial continues today as the country fights to fend off or delay the worst effects of COVID-19.

President Donald Trump and several Republican governors delayed action and failed to heed the warnings of the nation's healthcare science advisors, while leaders in other countries, such as South Korea and Germany, have taken more timely and successful actions.

A decade ago, Naomi Oreskes, a Harvard history of science professor, compared climate change denial to tobacco danger denial in her book, *Merchants of Doubt*, which was penned with Eric Conway and later made into a documentary film. The two then wrote a science fiction novel, *The Collapse of Western Civilization*, that explored a future where denial about climate science in Western countries kept them from responding to the climate crisis, while an authoritarian China did.

The argument about the role of government and its relationship to science remains tragically relevant during the COVID-19 pandemic.

"Eric and I had been talking for a long time about what we saw as a central irony in the story of *Merchants of Doubt*," Oreskes says. "And that was that the people we were studying, the people we refer to as merchants of doubt, [believed they] were fighting to protect freedom, that they were defending American democracy, American

"How Science Denial on the Political Right Hampers the US Response to COVID-19," by Adam Wernick, *The World*, April 22, 2020. Reprinted by permission.

freedom, and individual liberty, against the encroachment of big government. But the irony, we believed, was that by delaying action on climate change, they actually made the problem worse and they increased the odds that the kind of government that they hate would, in fact, actually come to pass, as we had to deal with the unfolding crisis. So, the idea was to write a story that would make that point."

When countries experience a large-scale problem like a pandemic that doesn't respect borders, a political system that centralizes power is better able to respond quickly than one in which power is more distributed, Oreskes says. "So, even though we might dislike centralized power in certain ways, there are certain kinds of problems for which centralized power is really important and may, in fact, be the only way to address the issue."

Until fairly recently, Trump was unwilling to use the authority that he has, Oreskes notes. When the seriousness of the virus first became identified, back in January, he didn't empower the Centers for Disease Control or the National Institutes of Health to mount a strong response. He also chose early on not to use such powers as the Defense Production Act to compel the private sector to manufacture ventilators, face masks or other necessary medical equipment.

"Now, three months in, he is finally doing that, and suddenly we see the private sector—GM, Ford—being enlisted to do this sort of work," Oreskes says.

Oreskes believes Trump's hesitancy stemmed, in part, from a basic conservative reluctance to enlarge the size and role of the federal government.

"In this case, the consequence of that reluctance is that the virus essentially went out of control," Oreskes notes. "And now, tens of thousands and possibly hundreds of thousands of Americans will die—Americans whose lives could have been saved if we had acted more quickly and with more organization in the early stages of this disease."

Conservatives have for 30 years been promoting the myth that there's no way to solve problems like climate change without succumbing to totalitarianism, Oreskes maintains. But, "you don't have to be a communist country to have an organized coherent response to a challenge," she says.

"The experience of South Korea, and to some extent Germany, as well, shows it's not about being totalitarian," she says. "It's about paying attention to evidence, respecting facts, respecting expertise, and then mobilizing the resources that you have in line with what the expertise is telling you."

What we're seeing now in the US validates what she and Eric Conway predicted in *The Collapse of Western Civilization*.

"Look at what's happening now: We've lost huge amounts of freedom," she points out. "The idea that we were somehow protecting our freedom by disrespecting science—we've now seen how bankrupt that idea is. I'm stuck at home and so are 200 million Americans. We've lost tremendous amounts of personal liberty, and we don't know how long this is going to go on. We've also lost income. We're seeing endless amounts of damage that could have been avoided if we had been willing to listen to and act upon the advice of experts."

South Korea acted on the advice of scientific experts early on, whereas in the United States, "we have a president who has shown his utter disdain for and disrespect for science," Oreskes points out. "He has been disdainful of the scientific evidence regarding climate change, he has been disdainful of the evidence regarding the safety of vaccinations against diseases like measles. And he is hostile to science."

"Many of us ... who do science, have been warning for a long time that if you undermine scientific agencies and the federal government, this will have consequences," she says. "And now I think we are seeing those consequences in a very, very vivid way."

In the 1950s and 60s, Oreskes notes, the federal government was not only putting a lot of money into science, but it was also "telling us a story about why science mattered."

"Why did the American people believe in the importance of the Apollo program? It's because we were told a story, a good story, a true story, about how science could help build America, how it could build our economy, how it could help build our educational systems and how we could do cool things like put men on the moon," she says. "So, I think we need to recapture that commitment to science and to scientific institutions and to scientists."

Equally important, Oreskes says, is to rebuild trust in government, Oreskes says. Science bashing has been linked in a direct way to a more general argument against the so-called "big government." She believes Ronald Reagan's slogan that "government is not the solution to our problem, the government is the problem," has been "deeply, deeply damaging."

"For 40 years, we have heard that argument made by political leaders on the conservative side of the spectrum, so much so that a lot of ordinary people don't understand why we even have a Centers for Disease Control, much less why we really need to count on them now in this current moment," Oreskes says. If the public is constantly hearing that government is bad or corrupt or inefficient, she adds, chances are they will begin to believe it.

"And the irony is that this can become true because, of course, if you put people in control of the government who don't actually believe in governance, then they're not going to do a good job in building the institutions that we need," Oreskes adds.

"We have a lot of dysfunction in Washington, DC, right now, and so people aren't wrong," she says. "People correctly perceive that Congress is dysfunctional, but that dysfunction is a product of 40 years of essentially anti-government policies."

The coronavirus pandemic shows us why the country can't wait until a crisis is upon us to mobilize the necessary resources, Oreskes insists. She uses military readiness as an analogy. Almost all Americans, she points out, accept the need for an army because we know that if we were to be attacked, we would be unable to mobilize an army overnight. "And we certainly wouldn't be able to build battleships and airplanes and aircraft carriers," she says. "We know that we have to do that in advance."

"We have a notion of readiness when it comes to military matters, but many of us don't have a similar notion of readiness when it comes to public health and medicine," she maintains. "And yet, it's exactly the same. If we're not ready in advance, we will not be able to protect ourselves from a viral attack."

If Oreskes were to write a story about how this particular crisis plays out, it would be a happy story about how it became a turning point and how, "because these issues became truly matters of life and death in front of our eyes, the American people began to wake up, and they began to realize that there's a reason we have government and there's a reason we have scientific institutions and there's a reason why we spend money preparing for crises that may not happen."

[Similarly], nobody knows absolutely, positively for sure exactly how climate change will play out, but we know that climate change will play out and it will be very damaging," she says. "And many of the kinds of damage that will occur, we can predict, even if we can't predict exactly when or exactly where."

Scientists in the US and China Collaborated to Fight COVID

Jenny J. Lee and John P. Haupt

Jenny J. Lee is a professor at the University of Arizona in the Center for the Study of Higher Education, and John P. Haupt is a PhD student at the same center.

T he US and China, the largest scientific research producers, are now international adversaries in the midst of a global health crisis. Since the new coronavirus was discovered, geopolitical tensions between Washington and Beijing in relation to COVID-19 have been appearing on major news outlets daily, and the US-China trade war has escalated to a looming "new cold war." Despite such turmoil, scientists around the world, including researchers in the US and China, are collaborating at a higher rate than ever before to address COVID-19, according to our analysis of SCOPUS bibliometric data.

Even before the current pandemic, geopolitical tensions were brewing as global rivalry between the two superpowers was steadily intensifying, and the decoupling trend between the two countries has been ongoing for some time. But experts have speculated that COVID-19 accelerated preexisting skepticism by the US, especially about the country's economic overreliance on China. And when it comes to SARS-CoV-2 itself, there is a high level of suspicion and distrust between the governments. While US leaders have referred to the new coronavirus as the "Chinese Virus," Chinese leaders have accused the US Army of bringing the virus to Wuhan. As an example of the international strain, the US director of the National Counterintelligence and Security Center told NPR, "we have full expectation that China will do everything in their power to obtain any viable research that we are conducting here in the US." US policymakers have also warned that cooperation with China is "a self-

"Opinion: Scientists in the US and China Collaborating on COVID-19," by Jenny J. Lee and John P. Haupt, *The Scientist*, June 22, 2020. Reprinted by permission.

harming exercise in a zero-sum competition for global leadership." US President Donald Trump ordered US withdrawal from the World Health Organization (WHO) for siding with China in its tackling of COVID-19, while China accused Trump of transferring blame for US's mismanagement of the pandemic.

In the face of such tense political rhetoric, China has enacted policy changes that may discourage international collaboration. The Chinese Academy of Sciences indicated that any COVID-19–related research publications must be evaluated by the government for "academic value" and "timing" prior to public release. Although its enforcement is unclear, this possible added review raised immediate international worries about future collaboration with China. More notably, China announced a major research-evaluation reform initiative in the midst of the global pandemic. Rather than basing researcher performance on mostly publication counts on Science Citation Index (SCI) journals, China is moving towards measuring quality mostly on domestic priorities, which also includes publishing in domestic journals. This move is predicted to lead to a significant decline in papers produced by Chinese researchers in international journals.

With the tense political rhetoric, policy proposals to limit cooperation, and widespread media speculation, one would expect a decline in scientific collaboration between the two countries. However, our research shows the opposite occurring. Utilizing SCOPUS bibliometric data, we found that the world's share of internationally authored science and engineering (S&E) research publications on COVID-19 from January 1, 2020, to the end of May was significantly higher than pre-pandemic S&E publication trends. Specifically, papers with authors from multiple countries made up 32 percent of the S&E literature on COVID-19 published in the first five months of this year, compared with 26 percent of the general S&E literature published over the previous five years. We also found that almost all of the countries producing the most COVID-19 research are, on average, collaborating with more countries per article on COVID-19 publications compared to science and engineering research before the pandemic. In other words, scientists are working across borders towards addressing the new coronavirus more internationally.

Regarding US and China specifically, our research findings indicate that the two nations are conducting the most COVID-19 research and continue to collaborate more with each other than with any other country. In fact, their rate of collaboration increased by 5 percent over their rate of collaboration on pre-pandemic science and engineering research. Furthermore, we found that the US and China have the highest rate of collaboration between any two countries with researchers from both countries having collaborated on 122 COVID-19 articles, which is 1.7 times higher than the two countries with the second highest collaboration rate, the US and Canada.

This growth in collaboration despite US-China strains actually predates the pandemic, according to our analysis of collaboration patterns between the two countries from 2014 to 2018. Our findings also debunked the so-called "China Threat." In contrast to Chinese researchers posing a threat to the US science and technology enterprise, collaboration with China was necessary for the US to sustain growth in research output over the five-year period. We found that when excluding publications with authors affiliated with a Chinese institution, US publications decreased by 2 percent between 2014 and 2018. Put another way, scientific collaboration across national borders is a positive-sum endeavor, despite political attempts to frame cooperation with China as being zero-sum.

In times of global crisis, it is imperative that scientists are able to collaborate and share data. Our research suggests that's happening in spades. Although scientists' international networks, and global science as a whole, are shaped by the resources, restrictions, and incentives that different countries provide, scientific collaboration is not determined by national interests or policies alone. International collaboration also occurs by the extent to which scientists respond. Right now, US and Chinese scientists are exercising individual agency in where and with whom they publish. Science, it seems, can transcend political agendas.

Foundations Must Help Native American Communities During COVID

Heidi A. Schultz

Heidi A. Schultz is a program manager for the Tribal Communities Disaster Recovery program under the Center for Disaster Philanthropy.

B uy two weeks of groceries. Work from home. Wash hands with soap and water. Many of the recommendations for preventing the spread of COVID-19 are difficult for vulnerable populations such as American Indians and Alaska Natives (AI/AN), especially those living on Native American reservations.

Housing on reservations is overcrowded, and nearly half of it can be considered substandard. It is estimated that between 35–40 percent of homes on the Navajo Nation do not have running water, and, according to the report *Closing the Water Access Gap in the United States*, 58 out of every 1,000 Native American households lack plumbing. Many AI/AN communities face food insecurity. Indigenous populations have a poverty rate of 25.4 percent, and on some reservations the rate is almost 40 percent.

High-Risk Population for COVID-19

Native Americans have many of the risk factors that put them at higher risk for severe illness from COVID-19. Heart disease, cancer, unintentional injuries, and diabetes are leading causes of death among AI/AN and lead to a life expectancy that is 5.5 years less than that for the US all-races population. Natives are twice as likely as whites to have diabetes. Native people die from diabetes at a rate that is 189 percent higher than that for other Americans. In addition, 28.6 percent of AI/AN under age 65 do not have health insurance.

"Native American Communities and COVID-19: How Foundations Can Help," by Heidi A. Schultz, *Health Affairs*, March 31, 2020. Reprinted by permission.

Health Care Infrastructure

Access to health care is often many miles away (sometimes more than an hour's drive), and limited transportation on reservations makes it difficult to go to a clinic or hospital.

The outlook for an effective and comprehensive response to the COVID-19 outbreak for this population is bleak. The Indian Health Service (IHS) does not have the medical providers, equipment, or facilities to treat critical patients. The IHS has 71 or fewer ventilators and 33 intensive care unit (ICU) beds at the 24 hospitals it runs. The National Indian Health Board (NIHB) surveyed tribal leaders, providers, and partners to assess tribal needs and resources. About half of respondents reported that the federal government or state reached out with information about COVID-19. Many respondents reported a shortage of personal protective equipment and hygiene products, several anticipated challenges to maintain adequate health care staffing, and some predicted the inability to isolate people who test positive for that virus. As of March 29, 2020, 165 Natives had tested positive for 2019 Novel Coronavirus, including 110 on the Navajo Nation.

How Foundations Can Help

Tribes expect that whatever help that is coming from the federal government will be slow to reach Indian Country and, with the many layers of bureaucracy, there may be little in the way of real assistance. Foundations can partner with organizations that have both the capacity and the ability (the infrastructure, cultural know-how, and access) to help nationally, regionally, and locally.

The Center for Disaster Philanthropy (CDP) has a COVID-19 Response Fund and has published recommendations concerning critical needs—particularly among vulnerable populations—such as personal protective equipment and medical equipment; getting necessities to quarantine and socially isolated individuals; access to medical care; and continued care of pre-existing illnesses.

Indian Country Opportunities

- The Decolonizing Wealth Project, Native Americans in Philanthropy, and the National Urban Indian Family Coalition launched the Native American Community Response Fund (COVID-19) to focus on needs of urban Indians.
- Grants to certain national organizations with regional and local "arms" will impact rural regions and Native communities. For instance, Feeding America and Meals on Wheels America can help meet immediate needs of Elders and others with food insecurity.
- The National Indian Health Board is a membership organization providing advocacy, policy work, communications, Indian health research, and technical assistance to Area Health Boards. Each Area Health Board serves a group or region of tribes and the related IHS facilities and services.
- Some tribal hospitals and/or clinics are self governed through Public Law 93-638 and are 501(c)(3) organizations run by the tribes.

  - Navajo Nation: Fort Defiance Indian Hospital/ Tsehootsooi Medical Center, Winslow Indian Health Care Center, Inc., Tuba City Regional Health Care Corporation, Sage Memorial Hospital, and Utah Navajo Health System, Inc.

  - Alaska: Alaska Native Tribal Health Consortium, Alaska Native Medical Center, and Southcentral Foundation.

- Some community health centers are located on or near reservations and serve a large Native population. Statewide, multistate, or regional associations of community health centers serve their member organizations to support their respective missions. For example, the Community HealthCare Association of the Dakotas provides clinical, human resources, finance, advocacy, and group purchasing support to 62 care delivery sites in 51 communities in North Dakota and South Dakota.

- Partnership with Native Americans serves 27 tribes of the Northern Plains and 40 tribes in the Southwest across 11 states with disaster relief, provision of food and water, firewood, coal, and winter fuel for Elders. They have completed the first delivery of essential food and supplies to Elders in the Northern Cheyenne Tribe, in Montana, and the Elders of the Crow Creek Tribe, in South Dakota. Many tribes have requested assistance for their Elders.
- Many community foundations are developing their own response funds.
- Funders may also choose to support rural regional health care centers that serve a high number of patients transferred there by the IHS.

Even when we are not in the midst of a pandemic, life for many Natives is difficult, and access to good care is limited. The problems are only amplified at this time. Action is needed now to support these communities.

CHAPTER 4

Can the Impact of Pandemics Be Changed for the Future?

Overview: How to Prevent Future Pandemics

Marisa Peyre, Flavie Luce Goutard, and François Roger

Marisa Peyre is an epidemiologist specializing in animal health. Dr. Flavie Luce Goutard is a veterinarian specializing in epidemiology. Dr. François Roger is a veterinarian and epidemiologist.

The international community needs to be warned that future pandemics could occur more frequently and affect the global economy with more devastating impact than Covid-19, the Intergovernmental Platform on Biodiversity and Ecosystem Services (IPBES) stated in a report published in late October 2020.

More than two thirds of emerging diseases and almost all known pandemics are caused by pathogens of animal origin. Such diseases are called "zoonoses" and, in the most impacted countries, surveillance and early warning systems, as well pandemic prevention plans, have been implemented in line with research on this topic. It's no small challenge—but, according to recent scientific studies, preventing disease spillover from wildlife costs 100 times less than trying to respond to such a disease once it has spread.

Experience shows that, when co-constructed and implemented in a participatory manner with local communities and decision-makers, these surveillance systems work. All that's left to do now is to invest in these systems on a larger scale.

That is precisely the goal of PREZODE (PREventing Zoonotic Disease Emergence), a new French-led international research coalition that was launched at the One Planet Summit. The aim is to construct an integrated approach to health.

But what is a good surveillance system? And what kind of difficulties are we facing in the field? Here are a few answers to these, and other, questions.

Effective Surveillance Requires a Multidisciplinary Approach

Surveillance and early warning systems have been created by studying how diseases emerge and spread, as well as associated factors that are mostly connected to human activities. These systems rely on networks of people that make health data available in real time in the advent of an epidemic.

One such example is the surveillance of Rift Valley fever (RVF) in East Africa. This mosquito-borne viral disease mostly affects livestock and humans. More than 30 years of research in that area has shown that RVF outbreaks in East Africa are correlated with the El Niño phenomenon, a significant climate fluctuation that affects the atmosphere's circulation on a global scale. In this region, El Niño causes abnormally heavy rains—an ideal environment for mosquito eggs to hatch, leading to a proliferation of mosquitoes that spread the virus.

In Kenya, RVF surveillance efforts have been strengthened during these climate phenomena. This allows for faster detection of virus circulation and better control of the disease. Such vigilance would not be possible without a multidisciplinary approach, integrating meteorological, veterinary and medical surveillance with livestock farmers playing a key role.

Input from social sciences has also been recognized as a crucial factor, highlighting the role that the public (farmers, livestock traders, hunters etc.) are playing in this process. These systems have been redefined around local knowledge and citizen participation.

Another example is the wildlife mortality reporting network implemented in the Republic of the Congo by NGO Wildlife Conservation Society, in partnership with national and overseas research laboratories and the Congolese Ministry of Health. Mobilising communities in the north of the country, this network works to detect the circulation of the Ebola virus.

Action Plans Initiated in Nearly All Countries

In Guinea and Congo, similar participatory surveillance networks that involve local communities are being developed, within the framework of the EBO-SURSY and EbOHealth projects. Work is also underway on the risks of disease transmission throughout the bush meat supply chain in Africa, particularly through the Sustainable Wildlife Management (SWM) project.

Furthermore, since the 2003 H1N1 crisis, many studies have identified the role played in the spread of avian viruses by live bird markets and poultry farms in Asia. Surveillance protocols have been established in farms and markets in South Korea, Bangladesh and Vietnam specifically.

Thanks to these studies, surveillance capabilities have been reinforced in many developing countries. All over the world, national action plans to combat pandemic risk are now the norm. Risk factors on farms are better known and the risks of spillover and spread connected to globalisation are better understood. Past health crises have also shown the importance of accounting for social and cultural factors.

To strengthen these collaboration efforts, particularly on environment, and animal and human health surveillance activities, the intersectoral and interdisciplinary "One Health" approach was created. But as the current Covid-19 crisis has shown, such early detection and rapid response still remain ineffective to prevent an emerging disease worldwide. Why?

One Health: Putting Theory into Practice

Despite several tangible initiatives in the field, the One Health concept is still too theoretical, both on the local level (participatory, community-based surveillance) and on the global level (big data, epidemiological intelligence). Strengthened international collaborations in reporting unusual, suspicious events were put to work when posts on social media began reporting "mysterious" cases of pneumonia in China in December 2019. But these integrated approaches still don't fully take the economic impacts of managing health risks into account.

A "good" surveillance system relies on three key factors. The first is risk characterisation, involving eco-epidemiological studies to identify virus reservoirs and sample to sequence the virus, in order to inform surveillance strategies. The second is participatory surveillance of unusual events, bringing together local communities and agents in the field to detect the first spillover cases and act quickly to avoid an epidemic. The third is the surveillance of animal supply chain (both wild and domestic), including markets. Alongside localised and rapid control, this surveillance needs to be deployed before diseases become epidemics or pandemics.

Historically, each crisis has been preceded by a series of more or less isolated human cases, as was seen with the repeated spillover of MERS-CoV to humans or avian flu in Southeast Asia. But sporadically isolating new pathogenic organisms that circulate in wildlife is not enough to prevent such risks.

By definition, the majority of recently-discovered viruses (H1N1 pandemic in 2009, the current SARS-CoV-2 pandemic) had never been detected before. This means that surveillance needs to be implemented immediately, without waiting for certain conditions and without targeting any particular pathogenic agent. Such syndromic surveillance involves monitoring the evolution of indirect indicators (haemorrhagic clinical picture for Ebola and Lassa-type illnesses, sales of antipyretics or drops in sale price of poultry for avian flu) in order to identify health events early on.

The Means to Act Rapidly

The risks of new emerging diseases will not recede after the Covid-19 crisis is resolved. What's more, the number of zoonoses is increasing, as is the frequency of spillovers. Accordingly, we need to be constant, implementing long-term surveillance, which comes at a cost. But that cost pales when compared to the impacts of an epidemic.

Setting up the Indonesian participatory system ISIKHNAS is estimated to have cost between €1–3m, with annual maintenance cost around €100,000. The system provides real-time reporting of livestock diseases and produces specific information needed by farmers (productivity advice, local health situation, etc.).

Early detection mechanisms are only useful when they result in immediate action, to avoid the spread of a disease. The emergence of SARS-CoV-2 showed the limits of the current approach and the overly long reaction times of international reporting systems. Restrictions (limiting travel, social distancing, systematic testing, lockdown measures, etc.) were implemented too late in the face of the extent of the virus' spread in China, then in the rest of the world.

Pandemic preparedness plans are only efficient if they are operational, with constant funds and materials, and with real-scale simulation scenarios. Establishing a trusted dialogue between scientists, politicians and the public is also essential if we want to act fast.

This is the essential role that international agencies such as the OIE, FAO and WHO now need to endorse. In economic and social terms, the decision to implement these plans is undoubtedly a difficult one, but a slow roll-out has far greater consequences. This is what the One Health approach needs to take into account.

Evaluating the Impact of Restrictions

In the fight against disease outbreaks, surveillance systems challenge is now doubly important. A pre-crisis assessment of the socio-economic impact of planned restrictions is clearly essential. But it is just as important to take into account the constraints of social acceptance of such measures, by considering the costs, benefits and impacts for animals, humans and the environment.

These two conditions are absolutely necessary to justify a swift call to action, when prevalence (the proportion of cases in the population at a given time) is still low, and show the advantages of long-term investment in proper systems, especially at times when nothing is happening. Obviously, these actions must be implemented early, without waiting for the next crisis to happen.

Over the past 20 years, studies on participatory surveillance of animal diseases and zoonoses have been undertaken all over the world, especially in the South. Strengthening collaborations and exchanging tools and strategies between countries is now extremely important, since we know how to develop these participatory surveillance and fast action mechanisms to limit the risks of zoonotic diseases emergence. What we need now is to implement these resources on a global scale.

Rapid Response Is Key When Battling Public Health Issues

Centers for Disease Control, Global Rapid Response Team

The Global Rapid Response Team (Global RRT) is a group within the CDC that responds to global health concerns within the US and around the world.

CDC's Global Rapid Response Team (Global RRT) is a unique resource that can rapidly respond to global public health concerns, both within the US and abroad. Since 2015, Global RRT staff have spent more than 36,000 person-days deployed in over 1,200 total mobilizations. Global RRT responses have included cholera, coronavirus, yellow fever, Ebola, measles, polio, mass gatherings, and natural disasters.

The Global RRT is a readily deployable team of public health experts coordinated from CDC Headquarters in Atlanta, Georgia, with dedicated full-time staff from across the world. We have more than 350 surge staff, with more than 50 ready to deploy on short notice. Some Global RRT staff remain in the field during an emergency response for up to six months.

The Global RRT:

- Responds to emergencies when and where they occur to stop health threats before they reach our shores
- Provides long-term staffing for international emergency responses in the field and at CDC headquarters
- Deploys field-based logistics, communications, and management and operations experts to support emergency response
- Helps partner countries achieve core global health security capabilities linked to the Global Health Security Agenda (GHSA) and International Health Regulations (IHR)

"CDC Global Rapid Response Team," Centers for Disease Control and Prevention, April 22, 2020. Reprinted by permission.

We Identify and Develop a Trained, Deployable,
Multi-Disciplinary Emergency Workforce at CDC

The Global RRT has dedicated staff, as well as surge staff from across CDC. Dedicated staff are hired full-time to work on the Global RRT, while surge staff maintain their current positions and mobilize when needed for emergency responses. All Global RRT staff become deployment ready (including medical clearances) and complete safety, security, technical, and contextual training.

We Can Rapidly Deploy up to 50 Public Health Experts
Internationally or to the CDC Emergency Operations Center

At any given time, Global RRT dedicated and surge staff are available to deploy to support or lead a range of emergency response activities. The Global RRT coordinates with other CDC experts who monitor and respond to infectious and non-infectious global health threats.

We Provide Stable, Long-Term Staffing for Emergencies
When a Sustained Agency Response Is a Priority

The placement of staff with experience in emergency management improves communication and coordination within the agency and between CDC and its partners.

We Serve as CDC's Link to Key Global
Health Emergency Partners

The Global RRT coordinates and partners with both US government and national and international partners who respond to global health emergencies. This includes the US Agency for International Development (USAID) Office of Foreign Disaster Assistance (OFDA), which is responsible for leading and coordinating the US government's response to disasters overseas. The Global RRT also works closely with the Global Outbreak Alert and Response Network (GOARN).

We Help Partner Countries Meet Obligations to International Global Health Security Agreements

Our work helps countries meet global health security goals related to workforce development; emergency operations; linking public health with law and multi-sectoral rapid response; and medical countermeasures and personnel deployment.

Why It's Important

The high-stakes Ebola epidemic of 2014 might have had devastating impacts on the United States if CDC and its partners hadn't been able to contain the outbreaks in West Africa. Public health agencies worldwide learned many lessons from the Ebola response, one of which is that we need a readily available group of public health responders who can deploy to control diseases from the moment we detect them.

Global RRT increases the efficiency and effectiveness of CDC's overall response capability by filling key positions in the field and at headquarters when emergencies occur. This improves global health security by increasing our ability to quickly respond to health threats and growing a stronger global emergency workforce.

Researchers' Understanding of Viruses Allows for Vaccine Development at Astonishing Speed

Anthony King

Anthony King is a freelance science journalist. He has written on a variety of topics in a wide venue of publications.

Six vaccine candidates in clinical trials for COVID-19 employ viruses to deliver genetic cargo that, once inside our cells, instructs them to make SARS-CoV-2 protein. This stimulates an immune response that ideally would protect recipients from future encounters with the actual virus. Three candidates rely on weakened human adenoviruses to deliver the recipe for the spike protein of the pandemic coronavirus, while two use primate adenoviruses and one uses measles virus.

Most viral vaccines are based on attenuated or inactivated viruses. An upside of using vectored vaccines is that they are easy and relatively cheap to make. The adenovirus vector, for example, can be grown up in cells and used for various vaccines. Once you make a viral vector, it is the same for all vaccines, says Florian Krammer, a vaccinologist at the Icahn School of Medicine at Mount Sinai. "It is just the genetic information in it that is different," he explains.

Once inside a cell, viral vectors hack into the same molecular system as SARS-CoV-2 and faithfully produce the spike protein in its three dimensions. This resembles a natural infection, which provokes a robust innate immune response, triggering inflammation and mustering B and T cells.

But the major downside to the human adenoviruses is that they circulate widely, causing the common cold, and some people harbor antibodies that will target the vaccine, making it ineffective.

Human Adenovirus Vectors

CanSino reported on its Phase II trial this summer of its COVID-19 vaccine that uses adenovirus serotype 5 (Ad5). The

"Vector-Based Vaccines Come to the Fore in the COVID-19 Pandemic," by Anthony King, *The Scientist*, September 8, 2020. Reprinted by permission.

company noted that 266 of the 508 participants given the shot had high pre-existing immunity to the Ad5 vector, and that older participants had a significantly lower immune response to the vaccine, suggesting that the vaccine will not work so well in them.

"The problem with adenovirus vectors is that different populations will have different levels of immunity, and different age groups will have different levels of immunity," says Nikolai Petrovsky, a vaccine researcher at Flinders University in Australia. Also, with age, a person accumulates immunity to more serotypes. "Being older is associated with more chance to acquire Ad5 immunity, so those vaccines will be an issue [with elderly people]," Krammer explains. Moreover, immunity against adenoviruses lasts for many years.

"A lot of people have immunity to Ad5 and that impacts on how well the vaccine works," says Krammer. In the US, around 40 percent of people have neutralizing antibodies to Ad5. As part of her work on an HIV vaccine, Hildegund Ertl of the Wistar Institute in Philadelphia previously collected serum in Africa to gauge resistance levels to this and other serotypes. She found a high prevalence of Ad5 antibodies in sub-Saharan Africa and some West African countries—80 to 90 percent. A different group in 2012 reported that for children in northeast China, around one-quarter had moderate levels and 9 percent had high levels of Ad5 antibodies. "I don't think anyone has done an extensive enough study to do a world map [of seroprevalence]," notes Ertl.

J&J's Janssen is using a rarer adenovirus subtype, Ad26, in its COVID-19 vaccine, reporting in July that it protects macaques against SARS-CoV-2 and in September that it protects against severe clinical disease in hamsters. Ad26 neutralizing antibodies are uncommon in Europe and the US, with perhaps 10–20 percent of people harboring antibodies. They are more common elsewhere. "In sub-Saharan Africa, the rates are ranging from eighty to ninety percent," says Ertl.

Also critical is the level of antibodies in individuals, notes Dan Barouch, a vaccinologist at Beth Israel Deaconess Medical Center and Harvard Medical School. For instance, there was no neutralizing of Ad26-based HIV and Ebola vaccines in more than 80,000 people in sub-Saharan Africa, he says. "Ad26 vaccine responses do not appear to be suppressed by the baseline Ad26 antibodies found in these populations," because the titres are low, Barouch writes in an email to *The Scientist.* Barouch has long experience with Ad26-based vaccines and collaborates with J&J on their COVID-19 vaccine.

The Russian Sputnik V vaccine, approved despite no published data or Phase 3 trial results, starts with a shot of Ad26 vector followed by a booster with Ad5, both of which carry the gene for the spike protein of SARS-CoV-2. This circumvents a downside of viral vector vaccines, specifically, once you give the first shot, subsequent injections will be less efficacious because of antibodies against the vector. Ertl says she has no idea of the proportion of the Russian population with Ad26 or Ad5 antibodies, and there seems to be little or no published data from countries that have expressed interested in this virus, such as Venezuela and the Philippines.

Simian Adenovirus Vectors

An alternative is look to our nearest relatives. Chimp adenoviruses were the focus of vaccine interest by Ertl for HIV and by Adrian Hill at the University of Oxford for malaria. "About one percent of people have antibodies to the chimp adenovirus, probably because of cross reactivity, which is why we use it," explains Hill, referring to the COVID-19 vaccine candidate ChAdOx1 nCoV-19, which has shown antibody and T cell responses in an early phase clinical trial. This candidate, which also encodes the instructions for producing SARS-CoV-2 spike protein, is now in Phase 3 trials in the UK, US, South Africa, and Brazil and is to be manufactured by AstraZeneca.

Unfortunately, says Ertl, use of the attenuated chimp virus in a COVID-19 vaccine means it cannot now be used for malaria, because those vaccinated for the coronavirus will have antibodies against the vector. But there are other simian vectors. In Italy, a Phase 1 trial of a COVID-19 vaccine with a gorilla adenovirus vector has begun recruiting healthy volunteers. Ertl says that having multiple adenoviruses from different species is "a good thing, because it broadens the range of diseases we could tackle." It could also allow animal virus vectors for COVID-19 vaccines to be used in places where human adenovirus immunity is high.

Not everyone is enthusiastic about vector-based vaccines. "Their reactogenicity profile is not great," says Petrovsky, meaning they stimulate a strong immune response. "Even [President Vladimir] Putin commented that his daughter had a fever [after taking Sputnik V]. Generally, fevers are a no-no for a vaccine." He says headache and fever have been relatively common in early results from vaccines based on viral vectors. Some people are prone to having convulsions from fevers, so extreme reactions cannot be ruled out, he adds.

Petrovsky says children generally react more strongly to vaccines than adults do, and that could be a huge drawback in countries with young populations such as India. "With vectors you are always trying to find the sweet spot," says Petrovsky, which is their Achilles's heel. "Too weak, and they don't work. Too strong, and they are too toxic." Petrovsky is involved in the development of Covax-19, a recombinant protein–based vaccine plus adjuvant that is in early clinical trials and was developed by his company Vaxine Pty in Australia.

So far, there is not much experience with vector-based vaccines on the market. The European Medicines Agency granted market authorization in May for a new Ebola vaccine that consists of a prime shot with an Ad26 vector, and a booster with an attenuated poxvirus (MVA). An HIV vaccine trial based on Ertl's research was to have started this fall, but has been delayed until next year due to COVID-19. "We don't have post-licensing experience," says Ertl, in relation to vector-based vaccines, "but these things have been in multiple trials, so we have a reasonably good idea about what doses are tolerated and about safety concerns."

A Measles Vector

In August, a trial in France and Belgium began recruiting volunteers to test a COVID-19 vaccine based on a replicating measles vaccine virus. This so-called Schwarz strain was weakened in the 1960s by serial passaging on chicken cells. The virus expresses the full-length spike protein of SARS-CoV-2 and has been tested in mice, say scientists at the Pasteur Institute in France who licensed the vector technology to Themis in Austria. It was previously tested on mice for SARS and for MERS.

It was shown previously that pre-existing immunity to measles acquired by infection in the elderly or vaccination in young people did not dampen responses to a Chikungunya vaccine based on this same vector. The measles vector "goes into cells, then makes more measles vaccine. It will come out again, infect more cells, but after a few cycles it stops," says vaccine scientist Christiane Gerke of the Pasteur Institute who is leading the COVID-19 vaccine trial. That the measles strain replicates distinguishes it from the adenovirus vectors and could explain why pre-existing antibodies do not matter. "So long as measles antibodies at the start do not eliminate all of the vaccine, then the vaccine replicates itself," says Gerke.

The live nature of the measles vaccine strain means that it could not be given to immunocompromised individuals. However, the Schwarz strain has about 50 mutations and measles vaccine strains have never escaped these attenuation shackles and caused disease in healthy people. "It is a promising candidate," says Krammer, though a little behind the others. The Pasteur Institute could not confirm whether volunteers had begun receiving the vaccine. In June, Themis was acquired by Merck, a company with a significant vaccine portfolio.

Success with viral vectors has implications for vaccine development overall. "It took a very long time for viral vectors to end up on the market, which they did with the Ebola vaccines," says Krammer. "The way I see it, this is going to speed up vaccine development in general." That is, as long as there is a successful outcome with a COVID-19 vaccine. Any misstep by a regulator with one of these vaccines could retard the potential of vector-based vaccines for multiple diseases, says Krammer.

Build on What's Been Learned from COVID-19 to Prepare for the Next Pandemic

Tiffany A. Radcliff and Angela Clendenin

Tiffany A. Radcliff is an associate dean for research and professor of health policy and management at Texas A&M University. Her research includes health economics, health policy, improving quality of long-term care, access to care for rural and other underserved populations, and improving care processes and outcomes. Angela Clendenin is instructional assistant professor of epidemiology and biostatistics at Texas A&M University. Her research focuses on risk communication, decision analysis, emergency management/emergency communications, cultural/social influences on communication/decision-making, and communications measurement and assessment.

While the world is still reeling from the COVID-19 pandemic, public health and emergency management experts are already preparing for the next one. After all, biologists are certain another dangerous new pathogen will emerge sooner or later.

We are public health researchers engaged in both leading public health disaster response and evaluating emergency management.

Here are five strategies that will give the world a head start—and maybe even help prevent the next outbreak or epidemic from blowing up into a pandemic.

1. Shore Up the Systems Already in Place

The identification in February 2021 of a new outbreak of Ebola in Guinea showed how critical surveillance and reporting are for rapidly responding to and containing infectious disease.

"5 Strategies to Prepare Now for the Next Pandemic," by Tiffany A. Radcliff and Angela Clendenin, The Conversation, March 8, 2021. https://theconversation.com/5-strategies-to-prepare-now-for-the-next-pandemic-154317. Licensed under CC BY-ND 4.0 International.

The process generally works like this: Once an astute clinician diagnoses a disease that is on the watch list of the World Health Organization and the Centers for Disease Control and Prevention, she reports the case to local health authorities to investigate. The information gets passed up the chain to the state, federal and international levels.

Clinicians, public health practitioners and labs all around the world send disease reports to groups like the WHO's Global Outbreak Alert and Response Network. It aggregates all that data and helps identify outbreaks of new infectious diseases and their pandemic potential.

If a pathogen does make it past local monitors and starts to spread, governments have emergency management systems in place to respond. These incident command structures provide a framework to respond to crises that range from infectious disease to natural disaster to terrorist attack.

In the US, various federal agencies have different responsibilities. They monitor emerging infectious diseases, establish a strategic national stockpile of resources and support the states in their preparedness and response. Responsibility for the emergency response lies with each state—that's in the US Constitution—so they have flexibility in how they implement everything on a local level.

One practical way to be prepared for a future pandemic is to ensure that all these systems and structures remain stable. That means maintaining funding, training and personnel for a rapid global response even when no pandemic threats are visible on the horizon.

2. Prepare the Public to Do Its Part

Effective pandemic response requires a clear, consistent voice and an actionable message that reflects best practices based on sound science. Messaging and data that clearly explain how each individual has an important role in curbing the pandemic—and that it might evolve as the pandemic unfolds over time—are critical.

The message to stay home and "flatten the curve" to avoid overwhelming health care resources with COVID-19 cases was an essential early public health message that resonated with many Americans who were not designated as essential workers. However, once initial shutdown orders were lifted and new treatments emerged, there was general confusion about the safety of public gatherings, particularly since guidance varied by state or locality.

Guidance is also most effective if it's tailored to different audiences. In the South, distrust of testing and vaccination efforts by government and health care providers is directly linked to language barriers and immigration concerns. One strategy to reach diverse and often underserved populations is to rely on leaders in the local faith community to help deliver public health messages.

Preparedness requires an "all of community approach" that engages everyone in the planning stages, especially those from underserved or vulnerable populations. Building relationships now can improve access to information and resources when the next disaster strikes, helping ensure equity and agility in response.

Science and risk communication scholars have started talking about the best ways people can manage the flood of information during a pandemic. Lessons from what's been called the infodemic of COVID-19 news—some trustworthy but some certainly not—can inform new strategies for sharing reliable info and fostering trust in science.

3. Get Coordinated and Practice

Emergency managers and health care leaders have long recognized that a coordinated response by diverse teams is critical for public health emergencies.

Tabletop exercises that simulate real emergencies help officials prepare for crises of all types. Like a fire drill, they bring together community stakeholders to walk through a hypothetical disaster scenario and hash out roles and responsibilities. These practice sessions include people who work in public health, emergency management and health care, as well as federal, tribal, state and local front-line responders.

Practice scenarios must also include the reality of "stacked disasters," like a hurricane or winter storm that puts even more stress on the disaster response system.

These exercises enable a community to test parts of the overall emergency management plan and determine gaps or areas to strengthen. Ongoing testing and training to the plan ensures everyone is as ready as they can be.

Beyond this training, health care professionals could be cross-trained to back up specialized clinical staff, who may need support over the course of a long pandemic.

The COVID-19 pandemic delivered lessons about infrastructure and supply chains. Strategic investments can shore up existing strategic national stockpiles of supplies and vaccinations for the future. If necessary, the president can use the Defense Production Act to order private companies to prioritize federal orders.

4. Polish the Playbook

After every major disaster response, all of the different groups involved—law enforcement, EMS, fire, emergency management, public health, search and rescue and so on—conduct what are called "after action reviews." They can improve plans for the next time around.

For instance, after the 2009 influenza pandemic, the Department of Health and Human Services found that while CDC communication efforts were widely successful, some non-English-speaking populations missed important messages. The after action review noted that distrust in the government increased when vaccine supplies did not meet public expectations. In turn, officials could plan exercises to test and tweak approaches for next time.

A thorough review of the response to the current COVID-19 pandemic at all levels will identify gaps, challenges and successes. Those "After Action" findings need to be integrated into future planning to improve preparedness and response for the next pandemic.

5. Build on the New Normal

Back when the 1918 H1N1 influenza pandemic unfolded, few Americans had a telephone. Quarantine rules led more households to use phones and hastened research that reduced reliance on human telephone operators. Similarly, no doubt COVID-19 triggered some rapid changes that will last and help the US be ready for future events.

It's been easier to adapt to the necessary lifestyle changes due to this pandemic thanks to the ways technology has changed the workplace, the classroom and the delivery of health care. Business analysts predict the quick move to video teleconferencing and remote work for offices in 2020 will be lasting legacies of COVID-19. A multidisciplinary team here at Texas A&M is tracking how robotics and automated systems are being used in pandemic response in clinical care, public health and public safety settings.

Some of the sudden, dramatic changes to norms and behaviors, like the use of face masks in public, may be among the easiest strategies to keep in place to fend off a future pandemic from a respiratory virus. Just as telephone systems continued to improve over the last 100 years, ongoing innovation that builds on rapid adoption of technologies around COVID-19 will help people adjust to sudden lifestyle changes when the next pandemic strikes.

Mistrust of Science Fuels Chaos During a Pandemic

Martha Molfetas

Martha Molfetas is a climate policy consultant and strategist based in Brooklyn, NY.

Scientists have been ringing the alarm bell on our climate crisis for over 30 years. They've also been warning us for half a century that new diseases and pandemics can come to fruition—from HIV/AIDS, to SARS and Ebola. COVID-19 isn't the first disease to break out of our disastrous relationship with nature, it's just the latest and most contagious one we've failed to control. Failing to listen to science has pushed us all into a reality no one wanted and none of us asked for. From the climate crisis to COVID-19, those who campaign against science back policies that cost lives.

As wildfires blaze through two million plus acres of land across the western US, we're reminded yet again just how fragile our pale blue dot is. Another year of record breaking heat. Another year of shocking hurricane systems, with two simultaneous hurricanes hitting the Gulf of Mexico this August and another five simultaneously active Atlantic systems spiraling around. Elsewhere in the world, 2020 has provided us with devastating Arctic and Australian wildfires and unprecedented floods that submerged 25% of Bangladesh—displacing millions. Record breaking heat has thawed our planet's ice caps and dislodged huge ice sheets in Antarctica, which could add three meters to sea level rise. Another year of climate records we're growing all too familiar with. Welcome to the Anthropocene.

For obvious reasons, this year is different. Not only are these climate events more chaotic and unhinged, it's all happening against the backdrop of the worst global pandemic since the 1918 Spanish Flu.

Here the US continues to hit stark records on coronavirus, while the President and other elected Republicans have gone on a COVID-

"The Anti-Science Agenda Is Killing Us," by Martha Molfetas, *Global Policy Journal*, October 5, 2020. Reprinted by permission.

denial misinformation spree. As it stands, globally we are not going to achieve the Paris climate goals. Climate impacts are harming communities near and far. We need to stop putting our heads in the sand, and start using science as the bedrock for policies that can help communities around the globe for our twin crises: climate and the pandemic. We can't build an economy that works for everyone without dealing with our shared climate and COVID realities.

Six months into this crisis, 208,000 and counting lost, and 7.3 million and counting cases here in the US; and you'd think we'd have a better plan by now, or at least have our priorities straight. American hospitals still don't have the PPE or the ventilators they need. There's no nation-wide mask mandate. Some governors and the federal government are seeking means to censor data and limit testing availability; all while spreading disinformation on supposed "cures" and the effectiveness of basic common sense measures to slow the spread—and Americans are paying the price.

It doesn't have to be this way. Countries relying on science to build pandemic responses have clearly come out of this far better than those ignoring science. New Zealand has basically eradicated the pandemic with less than 1,900 total cases and the longest stretch of no new cases seen thus far. A common sense approach led by listening to health policy experts and scientists works. A national mask mandate and lockdown works. Swift coordination of resources to buttress hospitals so staff have the tools they need works. Providing everyone with temporary UBI works.

What doesn't work are attempts to censor data, an uncoordinated effort to get PPE and ventilators where they're needed, no national mask mandate, misinformation on medications and masks from our leaders, and a sad one-time check to Americans coping with what's likely to be a year-long, or longer, pandemic. The US is not alone, Russia and Brazil's governments are doing similar things along the lines of misinformation and denial. Together BRUS, or Brazil, Russia and the United States account for 39% of all cases and 37% of all global deaths, that's roughly 375,000 lives lost from these three countries alone out of one million deaths. A damning club to be a part of: the short list of countries doing active harm to their citizenry for no fathomable reason other than political posturing and an opportunity to bend ever towards autocracy.

So not only are we seeing the last vestiges of a livable planet slip away. We're seeing just how dangerous an anti-science agenda can be towards our public health. The UN was right, if COVID-19 doesn't kill us climate change will. An anti-science agenda on climate and COVID-19 is not the answer and it never has been.

Somehow we are still funding massive fossil fuel projects with public money, not just in the US, but in all G20 nations to the tune of $71.8 billion a year as of 2017. This is obviously at the unique time where we are feeling the effects of climate impacts and the window for swift action is closing. Right now, 5.1 million people have been displaced globally by climate and environmental impacts.

Some countries are going above and beyond. The Netherlands is relying on coastal adaptation measures to protect communities and adapt to rising seas. Costa Rica continues to break records on clean energy use and reforestation. Meanwhile here in the US, the Republican-led government is advocating for opening up areas around the Grand Canyon to uranium mining, which would damage potable water supplies for the Navajo Nation and countless communities across Arizona. Not to mention, efforts to vastly expand offshore oil drilling and an acceleration in public land leases for oil and gas interests—all in addition to rollbacks on climate resiliency and emissions cutting efforts launched by the Obama Administration.

The IPCC's latest report reiterates the importance of keeping fossil fuels in the ground and investing in adaptation and mitigation efforts. But with fossil fuels still accounting for 80% of the world's energy at this crucial time, it's clear we're nowhere near close to doing enough. With one million globally dead to COVID-19 in just nine months, we're clearly not doing enough. What's missing from policy responses on both fronts is a science-focused agenda. We can all be like New Zealand on COVID-19, and like Costa Rica or the Netherlands on climate—or we can set ourselves up for more collective misery. Ignoring experts and propelling a "business as usual" approach to both issues isn't moving us forward, it's just putting us in a deeper hole we'll have to get out of later.

Vaccine Hesitancy Prevents Herd Immunity Against Pandemics

Kelly Elterman

Dr. Kelly Elterman is an experienced anesthesiologist, who is committed to education through writing.

Refusing a vaccine when one is available is known as "vaccine hesitancy." In recent years, vaccine hesitancy has increased worldwide—so much so that the World Health Organization considered it a top 10 global health threat in 2019. Misinformation is a major cause of vaccine hesitancy, and there is much misinformation about both COVID-19 and its vaccine because they are new.

We'll go over common causes of vaccine hesitancy and explore some ways to handle it, as well as provide some reliable sources of information.

Why Is Vaccine Hesitancy a Problem?

Vaccine hesitancy or distrust is a problem because it can make it harder to contain a disease. To improve disease control in a community, the community must reach "herd immunity." Herd immunity means that the majority of people cannot get sick or spread the disease to others. In this way, the whole community is protected.

The percent of people that need to be immunized to achieve herd immunity is different for different diseases. For COVID-19, experts estimate that between 70% and 90% of a community would need to be immunized against the virus to achieve herd immunity, although the exact number is not known. People can become immunized either by having a COVID-19 infection or through taking a vaccine.

"COVID-19 Vaccine Distrust: Why It's High, and How to Respond to It," by Kelly Elterman, Good Rx, February 9, 2021. Reprinted by permission.

Since COVID-19 can be a very serious illness, if 70% to 90% of Americans became sick, a large number of people would need to be hospitalized and many could die. This is why having a vaccine that works is so important. With a vaccine, many more people could become immunized without getting sick. If not enough people take the vaccine, though, achieving herd immunity becomes much more difficult.

Why Are Some People Hesitant to Get the COVID-19 Vaccine?

There are many reasons why people may hesitate to take the COVID-19 vaccine.

Distrust of vaccines: Some people will not accept any vaccines at all. For example, some people choose not to get the yearly flu vaccine because they think it does not work or they worry that it will make them sick. Others worry about links between vaccines and autism disorder, and although these links have been disproven, they choose to skip recommended childhood vaccines.

Vaccine timeline: Others may accept common vaccines, but may hesitate to take the COVID-19 vaccine because it is new and was created quickly. In the past, development and approval of most vaccines took years. For the COVID-19 vaccine, creation and approval took less than a year. This seems rushed to some, and may contribute to concerns about vaccine safety. However, development of the vaccine was not as rushed as it seems. Scientists have used the technology behind the COVID-19 vaccine for 20 years. This is why they were able to create the vaccine as fast as they did.

Effectiveness: While some people worry about safety, others worry about effectiveness. After development of the vaccine, scientists studied it in human volunteers. These early studies have shown that the vaccine is safe and effective, but there is still much that is unknown, including how long the vaccine is effective, if it works against new strains of the virus, and whether or not someone who is vaccinated can still spread the disease to others.

Side effects: Fear of unknown side effects and frustration about unknown long-term effects are other reasons that some people may not accept the vaccine.

Lack of concern about the virus: Finally, there are also some communities where people do not consider COVID-19 to be a serious risk. In these communities, people may not accept a COVID vaccine because to them the risks of the vaccine seem greater than the risks of the disease.

Why Are Communities of Color and Rural Communities Reluctant to Receive the Vaccine?

Communities of color may be more likely to distrust the vaccine because they have less trust in the medical system—which unfortunately has a history of mistreating them.

African Americans

In the past, African Americans were subject to medical experiments. For example, in 1932, the US Public Health Service started the Tuskegee Syphilis Study in Alabama. The study involved nearly 400 Black men and went on for 40 years. During this time, the men were never told the true purpose of the study and were not offered treatment for the disease, even when one became readily available.

Another example of medical mistreatment of African Americans is the story of Henrietta Lacks. Lacks was an African American woman who had cervical cancer in the 1950s. Her doctor sent a sample of her cells, without her consent, to Dr. George Gey, a cancer researcher. Dr. Gey soon discovered that Lacks' cells continuously doubled and did not die, unlike any other cells he studied. He named them HeLa cells. The study of these cells over decades has aided many medical discoveries, including cancer treatment and the creation of the polio vaccine.

Today, these cells are still being used to study cancers, toxins, drugs, and viruses. However, Lacks never knew that her cells were being studied, and neither she nor her family were ever compensated, despite the discoveries that emerged from her cells.

Native Americans

Other communities of color, such as Native Americans, have faced similar medical mistreatment.

In the 1960s and 1970s, the Indian Health Services forcibly sterilized approximately 1 in 4 Native American women under the guise of different medical procedures and without consent.

In 1989, the Havasupai Tribe agreed to allow the Arizona State University to study their communities' blood samples to determine if there was a genetic reason for their increased rates of diabetes. The tribal members who signed a consent form believed they were giving consent for the study of diabetes only. Instead, researchers went on to study and publish findings on several unrelated medical conditions, as well as the tribe's likely historical origins.

Experiences such as these led to understandable distrust of the medical community and any new medical treatment, including vaccines.

Not all members of these communities completely distrust vaccines, however. Compared to Non-Hispanic White Americans, only 10% of Native American children are less likely to be fully vaccinated against common diseases, and 20% of Native American adults are less likely to accept a flu vaccine.

Even the COVID-19 vaccine has support within tribal communities. Despite the centuries-old distrust of the medical system, there are tribal members who have volunteered for COVID-19 vaccine trials and have encouraged others to get vaccinated because they feel it is ultimately best for their community.

Hispanic Americans

Although they may not have the same history of medical experimentation, Hispanic communities are also wary of new medical treatments. This is because, like African Americans, they have a history of racism and discrimination with the government and medical system. Unfortunately, these are also the communities most affected by COVID-19.

Rural Communities

In rural communities, vaccine reluctance is due to misinformation rather than a historical distrust of the medical system. In many rural areas, particularly where local leaders have not required precautions, members may not consider COVID-19 to be a serious danger. Similarly, many rural community members view vaccination as a personal choice, rather than a community responsibility.

In other communities, members have spread conspiracy theories about vaccine safety and effectiveness. Such misinformation appears common in rural areas and contributes to increased vaccine distrust.

Why Is Vaccine Distrust Higher in Some Countries (Like Russia) Than Others (Like China)?

Vaccine hesitancy is a worldwide problem and occurs in more than 90% of countries.

Research on acceptance of the COVID-19 vaccine shows that vaccine acceptance depends on how much the people of a particular country trust the government. For example, vaccine acceptance rates in Asian countries where citizens overwhelmingly trust the government are close to 80%. In the United States, COVID-19 vaccine acceptance is around 69%.

In countries with low government trust, like Russia, people do not believe that the vaccine is effective and so the acceptance rate is less than 50%.

Why Are Some Healthcare Workers Hesitant to Get the COVID-19 Vaccine?

Healthcare workers share some of the same concerns about the COVID-19 vaccine as lay people, including worries about vaccine safety, unknown long-term effects, and the possibility of studies being rushed.

In a recent survey, 29% of healthcare workers were hesitant to accept the COVID-19 vaccine. It is important to remember, however, that the term "healthcare worker" includes not only doctors and nurses, but also those who work in roles requiring only a high school education. The same survey showed that those with a college education are more likely to accept the vaccine.

Additionally, 40% of healthcare workers are members of minority communities, which as previously mentioned are more likely to distrust vaccines due to a history of mistreatment by the medical community. Healthcare workers, like the members of the communities they serve, can also be affected by misinformation.

What Is the Best Way to Handle Misinformation Around Vaccination?

The best way to approach misinformation is with education and accurate, fact-based information. Here are some tips for different groups.

Community leaders: Provide correct information about vaccine development, safety, and effectiveness, and make this information easily accessible.

Healthcare providers: Educate patients and colleagues, dispel myths for friends and family, and stay up to date on the rapidly evolving science. The most important way, however, that doctors, nurses, and pharmacists can help their communities is by showing them that they accept the vaccine for themselves and recommend it for their loved ones. Providing people with resources for accurate information is important, but showing people that the leaders and healthcare workers of their communities accept the vaccine is likely to be much more effective.

General public: Be curious about everything you see and hear. See something on the news? Read something on the internet? Hear something from a friend? Check verified sources to see if they agree. Then, ask your doctor or a healthcare provider in your community what he or she thinks about it. If verified sources or your doctor tell you something different, ask them to explain why and then where you might be able to get more information.

What Are the Best Resources for Objective, Verified Information About Vaccines?

The World Health Organization, the Centers for Disease Control and Prevention, and the American Academy of Pediatrics websites are all excellent resources for objective, fact-based, and verified vaccine information.

Local universities, hospitals, and doctors' offices are also good resources for accurate and reliable information.

The Bottom Line

There is a lot of misinformation around COVID-19 and its vaccine. This misinformation contributes to vaccine distrust in many communities. Vaccine distrust can lower vaccination rates and make achieving control of the disease difficult.

The best way to improve vaccine acceptance is through education and example. With increased vaccine acceptance among healthcare workers and community leaders, people may be more likely to get vaccinated.

Partisan Politics Erodes Trust in the World Health Organization

J. J. Moncus and Aidan Connaughton

J. J. Moncus and Aidan Connaughton are research assistants at Pew Research Center. They both specialize in global attitudes research.

The World Health Organization, a specialized agency of the United Nations, has historically served several public health functions, including fighting communicable and non-communicable diseases. It has played a high-profile role in addressing the global spread of the coronavirus, which it characterized as a pandemic in early March. But in mid-April, US President Donald Trump ordered his administration to halt US funding of the organization, accusing it of making a series of consequential mistakes in its handling of COVID-19. On May 29, Trump announced that he would seek to terminate the country's relationship with the WHO completely and redirect funds toward other world public health needs.

Amid scrutiny of the WHO, here are key facts about the organization and how Americans see it.

1

The WHO is funded by the UN, other intergovernmental organizations and a slew of nongovernmental organizations and private donors. Funding is made up of both required (or "assessed") contributions from member states and voluntary contributions, which can also come from member states. In 2018, roughly half (51%) of the organization's total funding came from its 194 member states' assessed and voluntary contributions.

The total approved WHO budget for the 2020–2021 fiscal biennium is roughly $4.8 billion.

"Americans' Views on World Health Organization Split Along Partisan Lines as Trump Calls for US to Withdraw," Pew Research Center, June 11, 2020.

2

The United States was the largest contributor to the WHO in the 2018–2019 biennium, giving just over $893 million, or about 20% of its approved budget that cycle. The second largest donor was the Bill and Melinda Gates Foundation, which contributed roughly 12%. Other top donors include Gavi, the Vaccine Alliance; the UN Office for the Coordination of Humanitarian Affairs (UNOCHA); Rotary International; the World Bank; the European Commission; and other WHO member states including the UK, Germany and Japan.

It is not clear whether Trump has unilateral authority to cut US funding to the organization. Since 2010, at least 10 different federal agencies have sent money to the WHO. Prior to Trump's decision, the US was expected to make contributions equal to roughly 11% of the WHO's 2020–2021 budget. (More information on US funding of international organizations is available from the State Department.)

3

Just 46% of Americans give the WHO positive marks on its coronavirus response, though views of how well the organization has dealt with the outbreak are sharply divided along partisan lines. Whereas 62% of Democrats and Democratic-leaning independents say the organization has done at least a good job in handling the pandemic, only 28% of Republicans and GOP leaners say the same.

The public rates the WHO's pandemic response more negatively than that of national health authorities. When last polled in late April and early May, 72% of US adults said public health officials such as those at the Centers for Disease Control and Prevention were doing at least a good job, with a much smaller partisan gap in opinion (only 7 percentage points).

4

Overall, 59% of Americans trust information from the WHO regarding the coronavirus outbreak. Trust is highest among younger adults and those with more education, though differences by education and age are relatively small compared with those by partisan identification and ideology. For example, 86% of liberal Democrats and Democratic-leaning independents say they trust information from the WHO at least a fair amount, compared with 27% of conservative Republicans and GOP leaners.

Partisans are somewhat less divided when it comes to trusting information about the coronavirus outbreak from the European Union, which is generally trusted, and the Chinese government, which is broadly distrusted.

In his criticisms of the WHO, Trump has argued that the organization has been too trusting of coronavirus-related information from the Chinese government.

Organizations to Contact

The editors have compiled the following list of organizations concerned with the issues debated in this book. The descriptions are derived from materials provided by the organizations. All have publications or information available for interested readers. This list was compiled on the date of publication of the present volume; the information provided here may change. Be aware that many organizations take several weeks or longer to respond to inquiries, so allow as much time as possible.

American Academy of Pediatrics
345 Park Boulevard
Itasca, IL 60143
(800) 433-9016
email: use link on contact page
website: www.aap.org

Founded in 1930, the American Academy of Pediatrics is an organization dedicated to the well-being of all young children, birth through young adulthood. Read all about health issues including COVID and the COVID vaccine. Parents can find trusted information on this site.

American Medical Association (AMA)
AMA Plaza
330 N. Wabash Avenue, Suite 39300
Chicago, IL 60611-5885
(312) 464-4782
email: use link on contact page
website: www.ama-assn.org

The American Medical Association is the largest and only national organization in the United States that encompasses doctors and medical personnel. It is dedicated to improving the health of all Americans. Read about various medical issues including COVID.

The Brookings Institution

1775 Massachusetts Avenue NW
Washington, DC 20036
(202) 797-6000
email: use link on contact page
website: www.brookings.edu

The Brookings Institution is a nonprofit public policy organization that uses a multitude of expert researchers to provide trusted information on current issues. It supplies readers with a vast site that includes articles, blogs, newsletters, books, and more on a wide variety of topics, including COVID.

Center for Disaster Philanthropy (CDP)

One Thomas Circle NW
Suite 700
Washington, DC 20005
(202) 464-2018
email: use link on contact page
website: www.disasterphilanthropy.org

The CDP is a philanthropic organization dedicated to helping all communities recover from disaster. Find out how you can help, and learn all about disaster relief through webinars, articles, blogs, and social media.

Centers for Disease Control and Prevention (CDC)

1600 Clifton Road
Atlanta, GA 30329-4027
(800) CDC-INFO
email: use link on contact page
website: www.cdc.gov

The CDC is the health protection agency of the United States. The agency works around the clock to protect Americans against health and safety threats of all kinds. Find out all about how to stay healthy, how to deal with COVID, and what disease outbreaks are occurring. Sign up for a newsletter delivered to email. And check out its online museum.

Intergovernmental Platform on Biodiversity and Ecosystem Services (IPBES)
10th Floor
Platz der Vereinten Nationen 1, 53113
Bonn, Germany
email: secretariat@ipbes.net
website: www.ipbes.net

The IPBES is an intergovernmental policy platform that currently is joined by 137 world countries. This organization plays an important role because experts believe that infectious disease pandemics have their root causes in world environments and ecology of natural systems. The agency publishes environmental research reports on important issues and sponsors events, and its website has videos on valuable topics.

Kaiser Family Foundation (KFF)
185 Berry Street
Suite 2000
San Francisco, CA 94107
email: use link on contact page
website: www.kff.org

The Kaiser Family Foundation is a nonprofit, independent charity organization. Its mission is to provide trusted information on national public health issues. Read trusted, accurate information about COVID, COVID vaccines, health myths, and misinformation. This site has appealing graphics to get across vital news.

National Institutes of Health (NIH)
9000 Rockville Pike
Bethesda, MD 20892
(301) 496-4000
email: www.nih.gov/about-nih/ask-nih
website: www.nih.gov

The NIH is a US governmental agency and part of the Department of Health and Human Services. The NIH is the largest biomedical research institution in the world. The main goal of this agency is to promote health and prevent disease. Read all about a wide variety of health issues including COVID.

Vital Strategies
100 Broadway, 4th Floor
New York, NY 10005
(212) 500-5720
email: info@resolvetosavelives.org
website: www.resolvetosavelives.org

Vital Strategies is a global health initiative. This organization looks at COVID from the angle of social justice, economic equality, and health care quality as all of these issues play heavily on the circumstances surrounding the COVID pandemic. Read stories and case studies, listen to talks, and hear from experts.

World Health Organization (WHO)
Avenue Appia 20, 1211
Geneva, Switzerland
email: use link on contact page
website: www.who.int

The World Health Organization was set up by the United Nations in 1948 with the aim of advocating for the health of the world's citizens. This agency has dealt with many health emergencies, and that includes today's crisis surrounding COVID. Find the answer to any question about COVID on its vast site.

Bibliography

Books

Maria Bartiromo. *The Cost: Trump, China, and American Revival.* New York, NY: Threshold Editions, 2020.

Arup Chakraborty. *Viruses, Pandemics, and Immunity.* Cambridge, MA: The MIT Press, 2020.

Bob Gordon. *Life After Covid-19: Lessons from Past Pandemics.* Horncastle, UK: Banovallum Books, 2020.

Sanjay Gupta, MD. *World War C: Lessons from the Covid-19 Pandemic and How to Prepare for the Next One.* New York, NY: Simon & Schuster, 2021.

Peter J. Hotez. *Preventing the Next Pandemic: Vaccine Diplomacy in a Time of Anti-Science.* Baltimore, MD: Johns Hopkins University Press, 2021.

Heather C. Hudak. *Covid-19.* New York, NY: AV2, 2021.

Douglas Hustad. *Understanding Covid-19.* Minneapolis, MN: Abdo Publishing, 2021.

Ali Khan, MD. *The Next Pandemic: On the Front Lines Against Humankind's Gravest Dangers.* New York, NY: Public Affairs, 2020.

Sara L. Latta. *What Is Covid-19?* Mankato, MN: The Child's World, 2021.

Kara L. Laughlin. *How Has Covid-19 Changed Our World?* Mankato, MN: The Child's World, 2021.

John Micklethwait. *The Wake-Up Call: Why the Pandemic Has Exposed the Weakness of the West, and How to Fix It.* New York, NY: HarperVia, 2020.

Don Nardo. *Covid-19 and Other Pandemics: A Comparison.* San Diego, CA: Reference Point Press, 2021.

James Rickards. *The New Great Depression: Winners and Losers in a Post-Pandemic World.* New York, NY: Portfolio/Penguin, 2021.

David Waltner-Toews. *On Pandemics: Deadly Diseases from Bubonic Plague to Coronavirus.* Vancouver, BC: Greystone Books, 2020.

Lawrence Wright. *The Plague Year: America in the Time of Covid.* New York, NY: Random House Inc, 2021.

Periodicals and Internet Sources

Rachel Cohrs, "After US Failures on Covid, Congress Is Working to Prepare America to Fight the Next Pandemic," STAT, March 25, 2021. https://www.statnews.com/2021/03/25/covid-isnt -over-but-congress-is-already-working-to-prepare-america-to -fight-the-next-pandemic/.

Dante Disparte, "Preparing for the Next Pandemic: Early Lessons from Covid-19," Brookings, February 16, 2021. https://www .brookings.edu/research/preparing-for-the-next-pandemic -early-lessons-from-covid-19/.

Robin Marantz Henig, "To End This Pandemic We Must Trust Science," *National Geographic*, October 13, 2020. https://www .nationalgeographic.com/magazine/article/to-end-this -pandemic-we-must-trust-science-feature.

Victoria Knight, "Obama Team Left Pandemic Playbook for Trump Administration, Officials Confirm," PBS, May 15, 2020. https://www.pbs.org/newshour/nation/obama-team -left-pandemic-playbook-for-trump-administration-officials -confirm.

Dan Mangan, "Trump Blames China for Coronavirus Pandemic: 'The World Is Paying a Very Big Price for What They Did,'" CNBC, March 19, 2020. https://www.cnbc.com/2020/03/19 /coronavirus-outbreak-trump-blames-china-for-virus-again .html.

Scott Neuman, "In U.N. Speech, Trump Blasts China and WHO, Blaming Them for Spread of Covid-19," NPR, September 22, 2020. https://www.npr.org/sections/coronavirus-live -updates/2020/09/22/915630892/in-u-n-speech-trump-blasts -china-and-who-blaming-them-for-spread-of-covid-19.

Andy Norman, "The Cause of America's Post-Truth Predicament," *Scientific American*, May 18, 2021. https://www .scientificamerican.com/article/the-cause-of-americas-post -truth-predicament/.

Ed Pilkington, "How Science Finally Caught Up with Trump's Playbook—With Millions of Lives at Stake," *Guardian*, April 4, 2020. https://www.theguardian.com/us-news/2020/apr/04 /trump-coronavirus-science-analysis.

Joel Rose, "Even If It's 'Bonkers,' Poll Finds Many Believe QAnon and Other Conspiracy Theories," NPR, December 30, 2020. https://www.npr.org/2020/12/30/951095644/even -if-its-bonkers-poll-finds-many-believe-qanon-and-other -conspiracy-theories.

Peter Van Doren, "When and How We Should Trust the Science," Cato Institute, September 15, 2020. https://www.cato.org /publications/pandemics-policy/when-how-we-should-trust -science.

Sarah Wetter, "Lessons from Covid-19 Can Prepare Us for the Next Pandemic," *Forbes*, January 13, 2021. https://www.forbes.com /sites/coronavirusfrontlines/2021/01/13/lessons-from-covid -19-can-prepare-us-for-the-next-pandemic/?sh=55ef4b9b728c.

Index

A

Argentino, Marc-André, 89–92
Avendano, M., 114–118
Azar, Alex, 40, 85, 87

B

Barouch, Dan, 144–145
Biden, Joe/Biden administration, 104, 105
biosurveillance, 37, 38–39, 49, 59
Birx, Deborah, 34, 35
Bolton, John, 61
Brown, Garrett W., 93–103
Bush, George W./Bush administration, 59, 60, 62, 86

C

Calfee, Courtney, 29
Carlson, Tucker, 78
Centers for Disease Control and Prevention, 20, 24, 39, 44, 61, 76, 77, 78, 85, 87, 122, 124, 149, 151, 162, 164
    Global Rapid Response Team, 140–142

China, 14, 37, 49, 53, 56, 57, 58, 72, 75, 87, 88, 91, 121, 126–128, 136, 138, 144, 160, 165
Clapper, James R., 57
Clendenin, Angela, 148–152
Coats, Dan, 49
Connaughton, Aidan, 163–165
Conway, Eric, 121, 123
Cook, Nancy, 84–88
COVID-19
    and misinformation, 16–17, 74–83, 90–92, 119–120
    US preparedness for, 15–16, 19–22, 37–42, 43–46

D

Deace, Steve, 76
Deere, Judd, 87
Doherty, Tucker, 43–46

E

Ebola, 19–20, 22, 23, 24, 72, 137, 142, 148, 153
Ehley, Brianna, 43–46
Elterman, Kelly, 156–162
Ertl, Hildegund, 144, 145, 146

F

Fauci, Anthony, 34, 35, 71, 74, 77
#FilmYourHospitals videos, 79, 92
Fitsanakis, Joseph, 47–69
Fleischer, Ari, 86
Funke, Daniel, 74–83

G

Gerke, Christiane, 147
Gerstein, Daniel M., 37–42
Gordon, Susan, 63
Goutard, Flavie Luce, 134–139
Greene, Diana, 26–27

H

Harders, Sterling, 46
Harris, Douglas, 28
Haupt, John P., 126–128
Hayes, David, 91
health care inequities, 114–118
herd immunity, 106, 156
Hill, Adrian, 145
Hindu, The, 119–120
Horton, Peter, 93–103
Howard-Browne, Rodney, 91
hydroxychloroquine, 80, 81, 119–120

J

Jensen, N., 114–118
Jensen, Scott, 79

K

Kamenetz, Anya, 26–32
Kelly, A. H., 114–118
Kilkenny, Michael, 88
King, Amiri, 77
King, Anthony, 143–147
Klain, Ronald, 23–24
Knight, Victoria, 23–25
Konyndyk, Jeremy, 24
Krammer, Florian, 143, 144, 147
Kudlow, Larry, 86
Kulkarni, Mauktik, 71–73

L

Lakoff, Andrew, 19, 20, 21, 22
Lankford, Ana Maria, 47–69
Lee, Jenny J., 126–128
Lewis, Wayne, 19–22
Limbaugh, Rush, 76
Loge, Peter, 24–25
Lurie, Nicole, 24

M

Marshall, Tony, 46
McConnell, Mike, 52
McConnell, Mitch, 23, 25
McEnany, Kayleigh, 25
McGraw, Meridith, 84–88
Melchor, Lorenzo, 107–112
Messonnier, Nancy, 85–86
Mikovits, Judy, 80
Miller, Jason, 85
Molfetas, Martha, 153–155

Monaco, Lisa, 24
Moncus, J. J., 163–165
Mukherjee, Siddhartha, 35

N

Natarajan, Nikhila, 33–36
National Center for Medical
    Intelligence, 39, 58
National Institute of Allergy and
    Infectious Diseases, 20, 77
Native Americans, 129–132,
    155, 159
Nelson, Robin, 26, 27–28, 29,
    30–32
Nyhan, Brendan, 76

O

Obama, Barack/Obama
    administration, 15–16,
    23–25, 60, 61, 107
online learning, 26–32
Oreskes, Naomi, 121–125

P

pandemic "playbook," 15–16,
    23–25, 60–61
Pence, Mike, 40, 84
personal protective equipment
    (PPE), 33, 41, 43–46, 74,
    115, 130, 154
Petersen, Martin, 63
Petrovsky, Nikolai, 144, 146
Peyre, Marisa, 134–139
Popp, David, 23

Q

QAnon, 77, 80, 89–92

R

Radcliff, Tiffany A., 148–152
Reich, Justin, 30, 31
Renfro, Paula, 29–30, 32
Roger, François, 134–139

S

Sanders, Katie, 74–83
SARS, 21, 53, 153
Schultz, Heidi A., 129–132
science denial/mistrust,
    121–125, 153–155
science diplomats, 107–112
Starbird, Kate, 77, 83
Starnes, Todd, 79
Storzieri, Derrick, 47–69
Strategic National Stockpile,
    41
swine flu (H1N1), 19–20, 136,
    137, 152

T

"tabletop exercises," 21–22, 24,
    150–151
Tai, Katherine, 104, 106
Takash, Daniel, 104–106
Torres, Olga Lucia, 81
Trump, Donald/Trump
    administration, 15, 16,
    23–25, 34, 37, 39, 40,
    41, 43, 44, 45, 47, 48, 55,

60–66, 68, 72, 73, 74–83,
84–88, 89, 90, 91, 119–120,
121, 122, 127, 153, 163,
164, 165

U

US Biological Defense
   Program, 49, 50
US Food and Drug
   Administration (FDA), 24,
   82, 90, 119, 120

V

vaccine development, speed
   of, 143–147, 157
vaccine hesitancy, 156–162

W

Wernick, Adam, 121–125
Wilder, Dennis, 67
World Health Organization
   (WHO), 14, 16, 37, 59, 60,
   89, 90, 120, 127, 138, 149,
   156, 162, 163–165

Y

Yasmin, Seema, 83

Z

Zandi, Mark, 88
Zika, 24